Candle Making Processes and Formulations Hand Book

OTHER RELATED BOOKS

- Fruits & Vegetables Processing Hand Book
- Fruit Beverages & Processing With Mango Products
- Food Processing & Agro Based Industries
- Manufacturing Technology of Snacks Food, Namkeen, Pappad & Potato Products
- Preservation & Canning of Fruits and Vegetables
- Hand Book of Food Dehydration & Drying
- Meat Processing & Meat Products Hand Book
- Technology of Food Preservation & Processing
- Hand Book of Food Packaging Technology
- Agro Based & Processed Food Products
- Potato & Potato Processing Technology
- Technology of Maize & Allied Com. Products
- Technology of Food Processing Industries
- Technology of Sweets (Mithai) with Formulae
- Hand Book of Organic Farming And Organic Foods With Vermi-Composting and Neem Products
- Hand Book of Fish Farming And Fishery Products
- Hand Book of Mushroom Cultivation, Processing And Packaging
- Hand Book of Spices & Packaging With Formulaes
- Start Your Own Cold Storage Unit
- Hand Book of Bakery Industries
- Hand Book of Confectionery With Formulations
- Breakfast, Dietary Food, Pasta & Cereal Products Technology
- Hand Book of Modern Bakery Products
- Modern Bakery Technology & Fermented Cereal Products With Formulae
- Technology of Confectionery, Chocolates, Toffee, Candy, Chewing & Bubble Gums, Lollipop and Jelly Products with Formulations
- Hand Book of Poultry Farming & Feed Formulations
- Hand Book of Pig Farming
- Agro Based Hand Book of Plantation, Cultivation & Farming
- Agro Based Plantation Cultivation & Farming
- Agro Chemical Industries (Insecticide & Pesticides)
- Modern Bee Keeping & Honey Processing
- Technology of Modern Rice Milling And Basmati Rice
- Hand Book of Goat Farming
- Floriculture Hand Book (Flowers Growing Technology)
- Aloe Vera Cultivation, Processings, Formulations And Manufacturing Technology
- Hand Book of Dairy Formulations, Processes & Milk Processing Industries
- Milk Processing And Dairy Products Industries
- Hand Book of Dairy Farming to Produce Milk with Packaging
- Hand Book of Ice Cream Technology And Formulae
- Hand Book of Milk Processing Dairy Products And Packaging Technology
- Dairy Farming for Milk Production Technology
- Ayurvedic & Herbal Medicines With Formulaes
- Hand Book of Ayurvedic Medicines With Formulations (A Complete Hand Book of Ayurvedic & Herbal Medicines)

Candle Making Processes and Formulations Hand Book

Written By

EIRI Board of Consultants & Engineers

ENGINEERS INDIA RESEARCH INSTITUTE

4449, Nai Sarak, Main Road, Delhi - 110006 (India)
Ph: +91-11-23918117, 23916431, 45120361, 23947058, 64727385
* E-Mail: eiritechnology@gmail.com & eiriprojects@gmail.com
*Website: www.eiriindia.org & www.industrialprojects.in

PRINTED & PUBLISHED BY

ENGINEERS INDIA RESEARCH INSTITUTE

4449, Nai Sarak, Main Road, Delhi - 110006 (India)

Ph: +91-11-23918117, 23916431, 45120361, 23947058, 64727385

* E-Mail: eiritechnology@gmail.com & eiriprojects@gmail.com

*Website: www.eiriindia.org & www.industrialprojects.in

Distributors:

EIRI PROJECT CONSULTANTS AND PUBLISHERS
4/54 Roop Nagar, Delhi-110007
and
INDUSTRIAL TECHNOLOGIES, INDIA
Nai Sarak, Delhi-110006

ISBN: 9788186732625

Revised and Enlarged Edition

Printed in New Delhi (INDIA)

₹ 750/- or US $ 75

Printed & Published by Sudhir Gupta for "Engineers India Research Institute", 4449 Nai Sarak, Main Road, New Delhi -110006

Preface

The types of wax used in the construction of candles have changed greatly during the past few centuries. Today, substances are often mixed together to create stronger candles with higher melting points. In the United States, standard commercial candles usually contain 60 percent paraffin, 35 percent stearic acid, and 5 percent beeswax. Some candles contain small amounts of candelilla or carnauba waxes (from the carnauba palm) to regulate the softening or melting point of the finished wax. Beeswax candles are made of only pure insect wax and paraffin plus a small amount of stiffening wax. The wick is made of a high grade of cotton or linen. The material is woven (or braided) so that it will burn in one direction and will curl so that its end remains in the candle flame's oxidizing zone for even and intense burning. Often, wire-core wicks are used. These wicks have a wire center that allows them to burn slightly hotter than cotton and remain erect in the melted wax.

Decorative candles often use waxes other than beeswax and paraffin. Bayberry wax (or wax myrtle, as it is sometimes referred to) is derived from the **fruit** of the bayberry bush and has a distinctive aroma making it especially popular for use at Christmas. Non-burning wax is used in those parts of a candle—mostly the shells or ornaments of decorative candles—that are not intended to burn.

The book **Candle Making Processes and Formulations Hand Book** contains chapters on*: Introduction, Equipment and materials, Raw materials, How to manufacture, Candle making* *processes, Wax melting, Moulded candles, Surface techniques, Novelty candles, Chemical colours used in candles, Candle power, Waxes used in candles, Moulds and machines, Selected formulations, Coloured candles manufcture, Perfumed candles, Medicated candles mosquito repellent candles, Magic candles (coloured flame candles), Project profiles [wax candle (automatic plant), source of finance, wax candle (manual plant), source of finance, medicated mosquito repellant, candles, source of finance, magic candles (coloured), source of finance, automatic cylindrical candle making unit (coloured and plain candle) and source of finance], Imported machinery for candle making, Faults, Common sense with candles, Candle making plant, Smokeless candle, Mosquito repellent candle, Magic candle, Coloured flame candies (red, blue & green flame), Candle making unit (semi automatic), Candle making (non-drip), Candle coating, Suppliers of machinery, and Suppliers of raw materials.*

EIRI Board of Consultants & Engineers

CONTENTS

Various range of Candles and Candle holders

Sand Candles

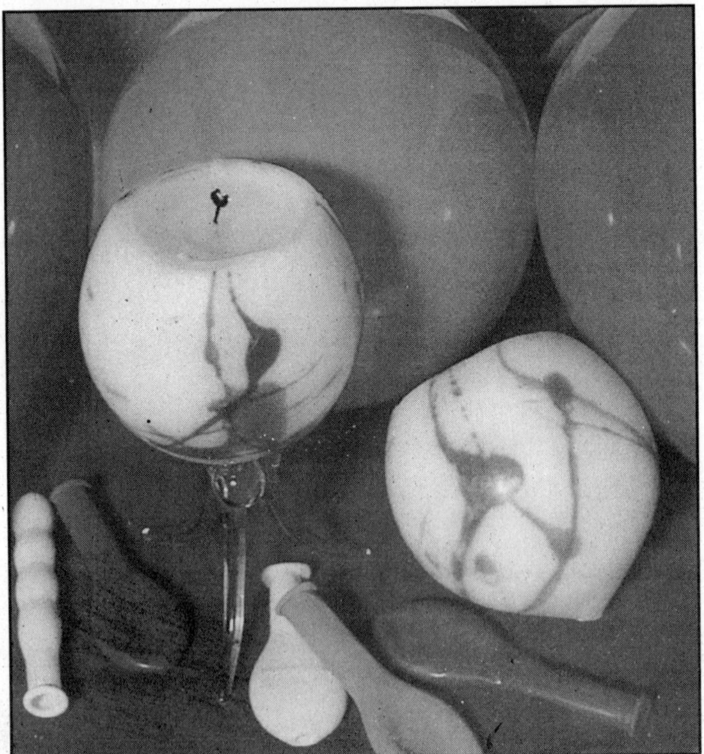

Balloon candles

Candle fruits can provide an unusual focal point for a supper table.

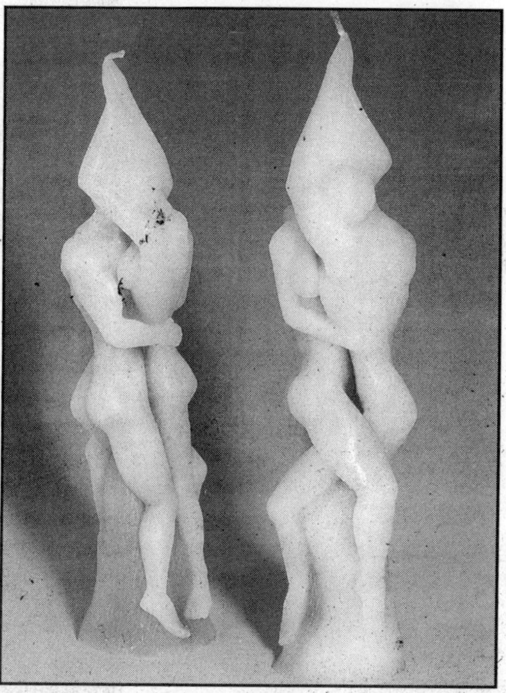

Opposite : Two moulded candle sculptures made by the pour-in pour-out method.

One colour & layered candles.

Land scape candles.

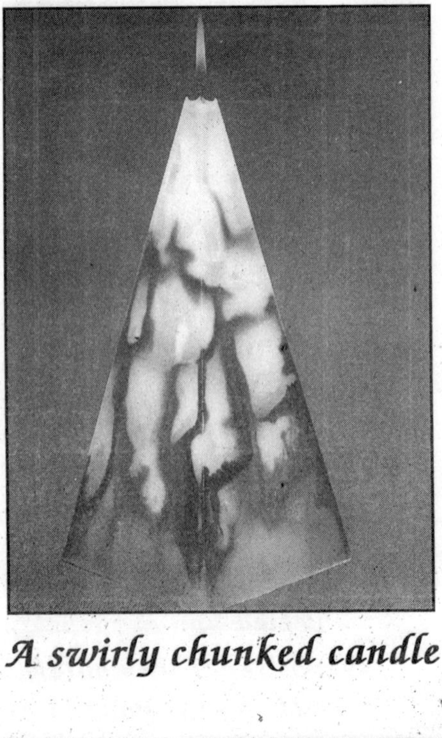

A swirly chunked candle

Coiled snake candle

Snake on a rock

Peeled banana candles made by the dip and carve method.

Chunked candle

Candle fruits.

holder
candle

A selection of pressed flower candles

A selection of appliqued candles

Snow flake pattern candles

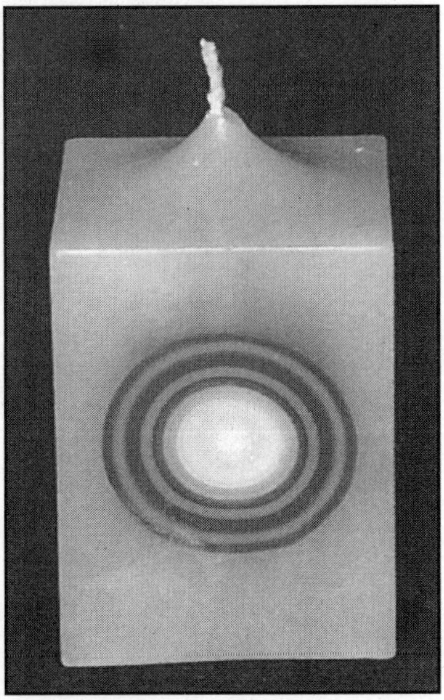

Ice cream candle

Bull's-eye candle

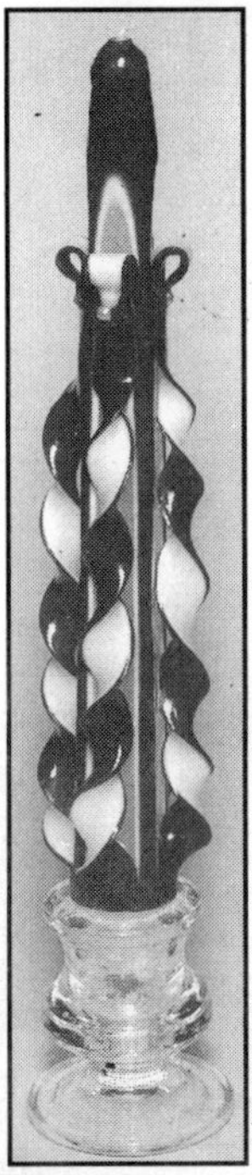

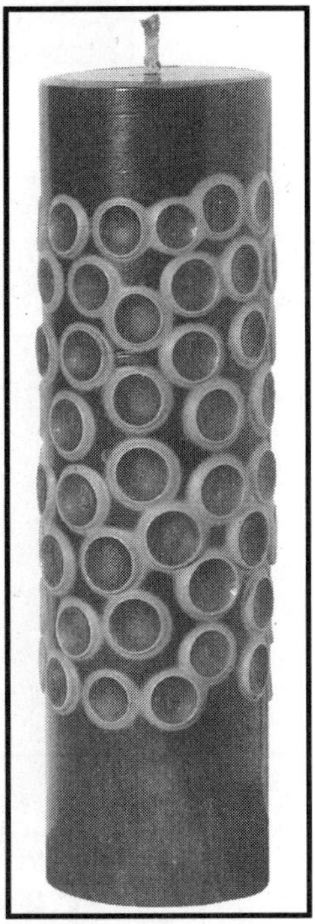

Cut and curl taper

Snake on a branch candle

Carved candle

Candles made by the dip and iron back method

Floating rose candles.

Collection of fungi candles.

Simple dip and carve candle

Star moulded candles with cut and curl corners.

1

INTRODUCTION

For nearly the whole of recorded history, candles have been the main source of artificial light in northern and central Europe. Further south, where temperatures are higher, people have tended to use oil lamps because candles soften and bend in the heat. An oil lamp uses a wick with one end dipping into a container of liquid oil, whereas a candle uses a wick surrounded by a layer of solid fuel and, therefore, needs no separate container.

Until the nineteenth century, tallow was the main material used for making candles. Tallow is animal fat – usually obtained from sheep but also from pig and cow – that has been rendered down and partly purified. Suet, much used in traditional cooking recipes, is a very similar substance. Tallow candles give off greasy smoke and an unpleasant smell when burnt, but they had the advantage of being fairly cheap and reliable. In 1860, the scientist Michael Faraday demonstrated this at a public lecture, when he ignited some tallow candles that had been recovered from the full of a wrecked ship. Despite having been submerged in salt water for fifty-seven years, the candles burnt steadily when lit.

Better quality, though more expensive, candles were made with different animal products, such as beeswax or spermaceti obtained from

The Art and Myftery of Making WAX and TALLOW CANDLES

the sperm whale. In fact, a spermaceti candle weighing about 75g (2¾oz) was made the basis of the standard 'candlepower' that was used to measure the strength of a light source.

Vegetable waxes have also been used, but in much lesser quantities. In China, wax was obtained from the seeds of the tallow-tree. In America, early settlers boiled up the berries of the bayberry bush and extracted wax from the residue. The desert shrub jojoba also yields a useful wax, and is now much in demand for 'natural' candles.

The first great improvement in materials came in the 1820s, when stearin was developed. Stearin is a chemical compound originally produced from refined fat, but now refined from palm-oil. It is harder than tallow at room temperature and produces much less smell. During the 1850s, paraffin waxes were first extracted from crude oil. The subsequent development of petrol-engined vehicles, and a vast industry to fuel them, has also ensured a steady supply of high grade candlemaking material.

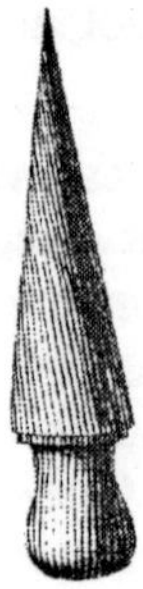

Tool used for piercing candles

The technology of candlemaking developed more quickly, and has remained virtually unchanged for the last five hundred years. The earliest candles consisted of a peeled rush dipped into liquid wax or tallow, and then allowed to harden. Such 'rush dips' were described by the Roman historian Pliny, and will have been familiar to countryfolk throughout northern and central Europe until quite recent times.

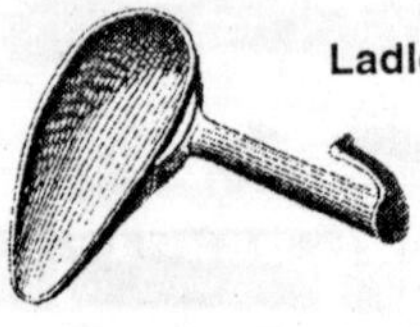

Ladle

The candle mould was not invented until the fifteenth century, apparently in Paris, and could only be used for tallow candles, because beeswax could not at the time be cast in reusable moulds. Beeswax candles, destined for churches and the homes of the rich, continued to be made entirely by hand. The extra labour involved added to the already high cost of the better quality material.

Knife

Before the advent of gas lighting and electricity, the naked flame was a daily necessity if life was to continue after the sun went down. In Britain, there were no olive trees to provide oil, but there were plenty of sheep, and that meant plenty of mutton tallow. Two hundred years age, every town in the country had at least one candlemaker or chandler. Their trade was tightly regulated by statute to prevent the sale of inferior candles and was subject to a tax on every candle sold. Not surprisingly, chandlers were often prosecuted, and imprisoned, for tax evasion. Also, making candles at home was forbidden by law and the penalties were quite severe.

Knife

It is hard to imagine the world as it was, when candles were so essential to civilized society that their manufacture and trade were legally controlled. Today, candlemaking at home is an enjoyable and relaxing hobby, non-essential but very desirable.

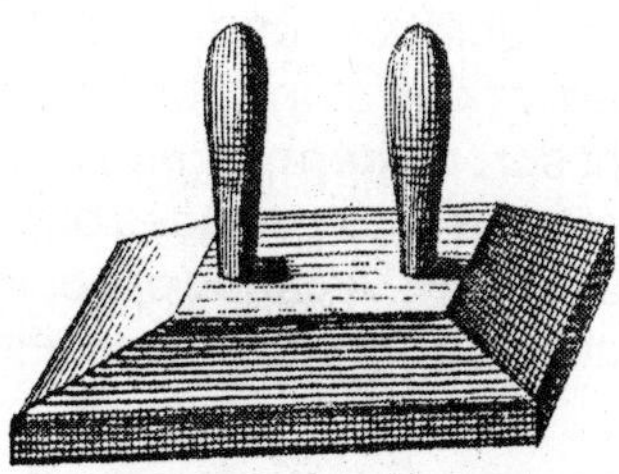

Tool used for rolling candles

2

EQUIPMENT AND MATERIALS

Equipment

None of the equipment needed for candlemaking is either expensive or complicated, and your kitchen probably contains some, if not most, of the bare essentials. Listed here are the items that you will need.

Thermometer

If you want to make good candles, then make sure that you have a thermometer. Waxes melt at particular temperatures, and remain liquid whilst

A selection of equipment used; for candlemaking: thermometers; double boiler; dipping can; weighing scales; measuring jug; wicking needles; washing-up bowl.

they get much hotter, but their inner structure changes. It is impossible to guess the temperature of liquid wax and, therefore, the only way that you can be sure that your are working at the correct temperature, and get good results, is to use the right sort of thermometer. A clinical thermometer from the bathroom cabinet is of no use, as you need one that is calibrated between 38°C (100°F) and 180°C (356°F). A candy or cooking thermometer is ideal, and these are widely available from craft shops and kitchen-ware suppliers.

Double boiler

This should be made of stainless steel or aluminium, and the upper part should have a capacity of at least 3 liters (5¼pt). If necessary, then you can use one saucepan standing inside another, although this will result in uneven heating of the wax and you will have to take extra care in matching temperatures.

Dipping can

This is a tall cylindrical container used for holding liquid wax. Professional dipping cans are made of metal and have a wide rim so that they can be held in frames for multiple dipping.

Weighing scales

Ordinary kitchen scales are ideal for weighing materials.

Measuring flask or jug

This is needed for determining the capacity of a mould. Fill the mould with water, then pour it into the flask. For each 100cm^3 ($\frac{1}{5}$pt) of water, allow 90g (3¼oz) of solid wax.

Wicking needles

These are steel needles 10–25cm (4–10in) long. They are very useful for inserting wicks and for securing the wick at the base of the mould.

Bowls

Washing-up bowls are ideal and you may need more than one. A bowl of hot water is used to keep dipping cans at the right temperature, whilst cold water is used as a water bath to speed up the cooling process.

Heat

You will need a source of heat for melting the wax. An ordinary domestic cooker (gas or electric) is ideal. Try to work as close as possible to your heat source, because wax loses heat quite quickly when it is carried about.

Candle made from a mixture of paraffin wax and stearin.

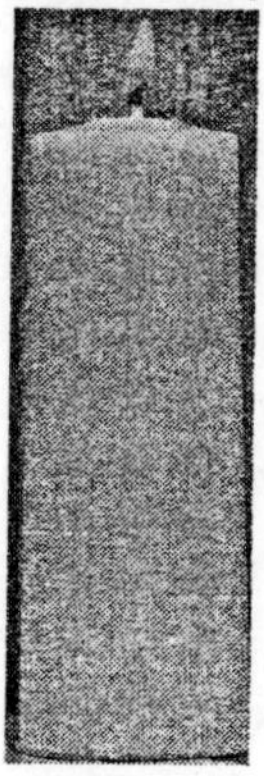

Materials

To make a candle you need wax and a wick. Both are available from craft shops and specialist suppliers. There is a range of waxes available, some of which have a variety of applications whilst others have very specific uses. Wicks are more straightforward, as they are all manufactured to an internationally recognized set of standard sizes. For making coloured or scented candles, specially prepared wax dyes and perfumes can be obtained.

Waxes

Paraffin waxes : These are colourless, odourless waxes produced as a by-product of oil refining. They are all solid at normal room temperature and melt at temperatures between 40°C (104°F) and 71°C (160°F). The ones most suitable for candlemaking melt in the range 57–60°C (135–140°F). Paraffin waxes for candlemaking are available either in pure form, or with 10 per cent stearin already added.

Stearin : This is a hardish white wax that is used mainly as an additive to paraffin wax to increase the amount of shrinkage in moulded candles. One great advantage of stearin is that the transformation from solid to liquid and back is almost instantaneous. There is no sticky in-between state. As a result, stearin makes a superb clear overdip that after twenty-four hours matures to a lovely crystalline finish.

Beeswax : This is a wholly natural product available in bleached white or untreated shades of brown. Beeswax is quite expensive but has a beautiful aroma. It is normally used in combination with other waxes. Modern church candles contain 25 per cent beeswax. Added to paraffin wax in quantities as small as 1 per cent, beeswax will increase the burning time of a candle. If more than 10 per cent beeswax is used in a moulded candle, then a release agent must be applied to the mould beforehand.

Micro waxes : Also a by-product of the petroleum industry, these are used as additives to alter the appearance and behaviour of paraffin wax. Micro soft is a tough, pliable wax that is the main ingredient of modelling wax. Micro hard is a brittle wax that is used in very small quantities (less than 1 per cent) to improve burning time and surface finish.

Overdipping wax : A blend of waxes and resins, this is used to give candles a tough, shiny and opaque coating.

Water candle wax : This is a specially blended wax for making exciting and expressive candles.

Dip and carve wax : This is a blend of waxes specially formulated for use with this technique.

A selection of materials used for candlemaking. 1. Dip and carve wax. 2. Water candle wax. 3. Paraffin wax. 4. Beeswax. 5. Stearin 6. Beeswax chips. 7. Beeswax sheets. 8. Wax perfumes. 9. Micro hard wax. 10. Plastic additive. 11. Wicks in various sizes. 12. Overdipping wax. 13. Vybar. 14. Micro soft wax. 15. Mould seal. 16. Wax dyes.

Plastic additive : This is an opaque substance used in small quantities (5 per cent or less) to increase burning time and improve appearance. It has a high melting point and must be added slowly to wax at 104°C (219°F).

Vybar : This is a proprietary additive used to increase the opacity of wax.

Wax glue : This is a soft, sticky wax used to glue two pieces of wax together.

Mould seal : This is a putty-like substance used to secure the wick in the mould and to prevent any leakage of molten wax.

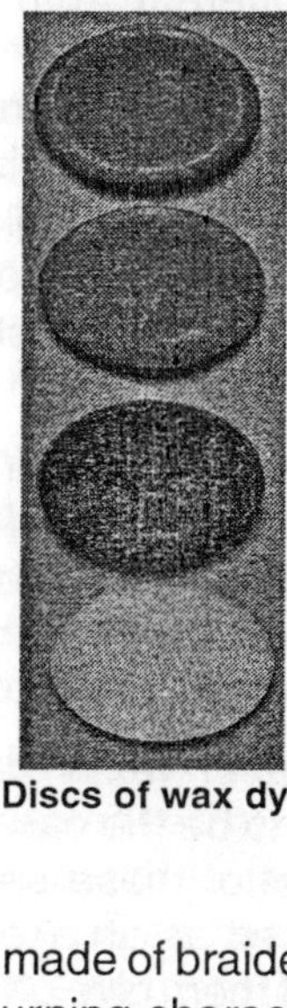

Discs of wax dye.

Wicks

These are generally made of braided cotton and have been chemically treated to improve their burning characteristics. The wick is only a means to an end, as it is wax vapour that actually burns, the wick merely delivering the liquid wax to the flame.

The size of the wick is determined by the diameter of the finished candle. Wicks are available in 1.25cm (½in) graduations. For paraffin wax, a 1.25cm (½in) wick is suitable for a 1.25cm (½in) candle, a 2.5cm (1in) wick for a 2.5cm (1in) candle, and so on. Beeswax is more viscous than paraffin wax, and beeswax candles therefore need a wick one size larger if ordinary wicks are to be used. Round wicks are best for beeswax candles and also for tall pillar candles made of paraffin wax.

Colours and perfumes

One of the great beauties of candlemaking is that wax can be dyed an infinite variety of shades and colours. You can use all sorts of substances to colour wax, such as crayons or poster paints. However, it is very important to use only wax-soluble substances. If other substances are used, then small particles will clog the wick of the candle causing it to sputter and go out.

Specially prepared wax dyes are the most convenient source of colours for candlemakers. These normally come in disc form for ease of division. Instructions for the proportion of dye to wax are supplied, but it is normally 20g (1disc) to 2kg (4lb 6oz) of wax. For overdipping, dye should be used at four times normal strength. Do not be afraid to experiment with mixing dyes, or use them at strengths different from that recommended, but remember that wax dye only shows its true colour when the wax has cooled and hardened. When getting the right colour is crucial, mix a test batch the day before. If the colour is right, then you can melt down the wax and reuse it. If the colour is wrong, then you did the right thing by testing it. For really bright colours, paraffin wax needs the addition of a small amount of fat – beeswax and stearin both provide this. For pastel shades, 1 per cent of wax whitener should be used.

Wax pigments, which come in chip form, can also be used for colouring candles. Their main quality is that they do not fade, and they tend to be used for special techniques such as applique and dip and carve, as well as for adding final touches of colour to finished candles. As they are not wax-soluble, they should not be used to obtain a solid colour throughout a candle.

One of the advantages of paraffin wax is that it burns with hardly any smell. However, this does not have to be the case. A variety of special wax perfumes is available, and the best of these use natural fruit and flower essences. Essential oils can be used as an alternative to wax perfumes, although care is needed as some of them give off a nasty, bitter smell when burnt.

3

RAW MATERIALS

The Fuel of paraffin wax candles was produced from bees wax spermaceti, and stearin and on account of the high cost the use of candles was confined to churches and households of the wealthy class.

Now a days most of the candles produced by the industry are made from a mixture of several ingredients. These are paraffin wax, stearic acid (stearine), small quantities of other waxes are added usually for the sake of appearance. This mixture, which can be used in all methods of making candles, will prove most suitable for nearly all projects. However, details of other materials which can be used are given as under.

Paraffin Wax

Paraffin wax is obtained by distillation of coal and shales oil and semirefined grades are used by most candle makers. It is usually available in the form of large blocks of petrol refining companies. For the several grades available the melting point varies between 50° and 70°C. For temperate climates the grade having 58° melting point is considered to be suitable but in tropical climate the grade having a higher melting point would be necessary.

Stearine

Stearine is a major compound of many animal and vegetable fats and is supplied in flakes by oil and chemical companies. It is added to the wax to improve burning qualities and also to help in easier removal of the finished candle from the mould. It is also reduces the smoke produced by the candle flame. Between 5 per cent and 50 per cent of stearine can be used depending upon the quality of the candle required. Ten per cent is generally used. Two factors should be considered, if high percentage is used better quality of the candle is produced, but stearine is an expensive material.

Micro-Crystalline Wax

This wax is highly refined byproduct of the coal and petroleum industries. It deposits a hard coating on the surface of the candle which improves the appearance by giving it a shiny surface and is hard enough to be resistant to minor damage. Because it is very expensive, this wax should be used in small quantities. Not more than 2 per cent is required to produce a good quality candle. While adopting very simple methods of candle making it is not usually required.

Tallow

Tallow is made from melted down animal fat and is rarely used in the present day manufacture of candles because it has a greasy touch, creates an unpleasant odour on burning and gives less light as compared to wax based candles.

Beeswax

Beeswax is obtained by melting the honeycomb of the beehive in hot water, straining it and allowing it to cool. At this stage it has brownish-yellow colour, and it is bleached before using for making candles. While it is an excellent material for candle making it would be uneconomical for making common candle because of its cost. It is available in the market in the form of flakes.

Vegetable Waxes

Many waxes are available in the market, present in or on the leaves of various plants and trees and can be extracted by melting off in bot water. Only a few can be mentioned here, though many others would be suitable for candles refered to here before.

These waxes occure as a coating or a top layer which acts as a protective media to reduce evaporation of moisture from the plants in tropical and dry regions. The important vegetable waxes of a much importance are Carnauba wax, Candellila wax, Quricury wax, Sugarcane wax, Rice bran oil wax, Tea wax, Japan wax, Esparto grass wax, Flax wax, and cotton wax.

The Wick

The wick is used originally in candles was of bleached twisted cotton yarn. Modern wicks are woven into a flat braid. This has the advantage that it is uniform and it curls as it burns. The curling the ends of the wick into the hottest part of the candle flame where it burns with complete combustion and the candle is consumed. In this way the exposed length of wick, and the flame height is kept constant.

Braided wick requires special machinery for its production and would normally be obtained from suppliers who already have substantial candle making industries. It is normally specified by the number of piles.

After braiding, the wick is treated chemically : bleached, then mordanated in solution of ammonium phosphate ammonium sulphate, ammonium chloride, borax and pottassium nitrate.

Because wick size is always fixed by experiments trail, the following is only a rough guide to the selection of wick size.

Candle diameter (cm.)	*Size of wick (ply.)*
2.5 to 5	15
5 to 7	24
over 7	30
Tapers	24 to 30

4

HOW TO MANUFACTURE

We always considered candlemaking to be rather like cookery. In both cases, a few simple techniques are combined to produce endless variety. Success in either field of endeavour depends upon the same critical factors; the right ingredients, accurate measurement, and precise control of temperature and timing. Equally important are liberal doses of patience and practice. The old proverb is true – practice does make perfect.

Melting wax and priming wicks are the two most essential skills in candlemaking, so it is worth taking time to become fully acquainted with them.

Working with heat

Most candlemaking, and virtually of all the candles described in this book, involve the use of molten, liquid wax. There are two ways of melting wax – a safe way and a less safe way.

The safe way is to use a double boiler, and for most candles this is perfectly adequate. The disadvantage of a double boiler is that it will not heat wax above the boiling-point of water, which is 100°C (212°F). However, a few of the candles described later in the book require wax to be heated above this temperature, and in these cases the wax must be heated in an open pan. Please be very careful when doing this and always heat was gently. Monitor the temperature carefully and do not let the wax overheat.

Priming Wicks

At the heart of every good candle is a good wick. If the wick is not right, then the finished candle will not burn correctly. You will always need a length of wick about 5cm (2in) longer than the candle you are making. If in doubt then be generous, as an overlong wick can always be trimmed. The instructions for each candle will tell you what grade of wick to use.

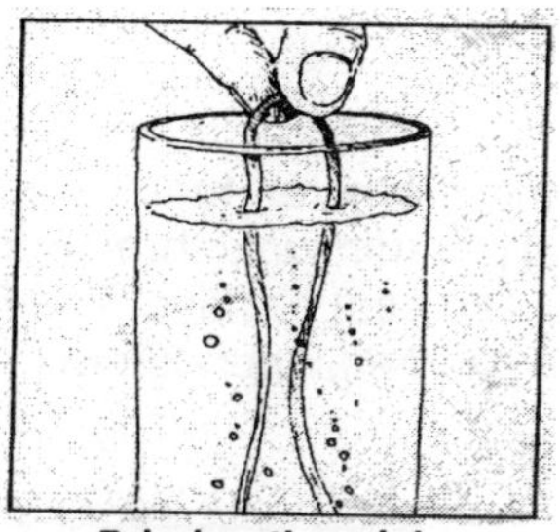

Priming the wick

How to – priming wicks

EQUIPMENT AND MATERIALS

Double boiler; thermometer; grease-proof paper in a baking tray; nail; 1kg (2lb 3oz) paraffin wax; three 60cm (24in) lengths of 1.25cm (½in) wick.

METHOD

1. Heat the wax gently until it reaches 71°C (160°F), then switch off the heat.
2. Fold a length of wick in half and, holding it by the middle, dip it into the molten wax for one minute. This forces out any air or moisture. Leave the thermometer in the wax whilst you work and note how long the wax holds its temperature. This will give you some idea of how often you need to re-heat wax when working at a constant temperature.
3. Remove the pair of wicks and straighten them with your fingers.
4. Hang the wicks over a nail to cool.
5. Whilst it is still liquid, pour the wax on to sheets of grease-proof paper to cool. When it has solidified it can be stored for later use.

Dipping

The simplest method of making a candle is to repeat the wick priming process over and over again. By repeatedly dipping the wick into the molten wax, you can build up a candle to any thickness you want. Dipped candles have a characteristic tapering shape, hence the name 'tapers' for candles made in this way.

For ease of handling, candles are usually dipped in pairs and are separated only when they have cooled completely. When hanging dipped candles to cool, make sure that they do not touch each other whilst the surface layers are still sticky. Hanging them over two nails, rather than just one, is an easy way to keep them apart.

How to – dipped candles

EQUIPMENT AND MATERIALS

Large saucepan; thermometer; metal dipping can at least 30cm (12in) tall; knife; 3kg (6lb 10oz) paraffin wax; three 60cm (24in) lengths of 1.25cm (½in) wick; 60g (approx. 3 discs) red dye. These materials are sufficient to make six coloured table candles, each 25cm (10in) tall and 1.2–1.9cm (½–¾in) in diameter.

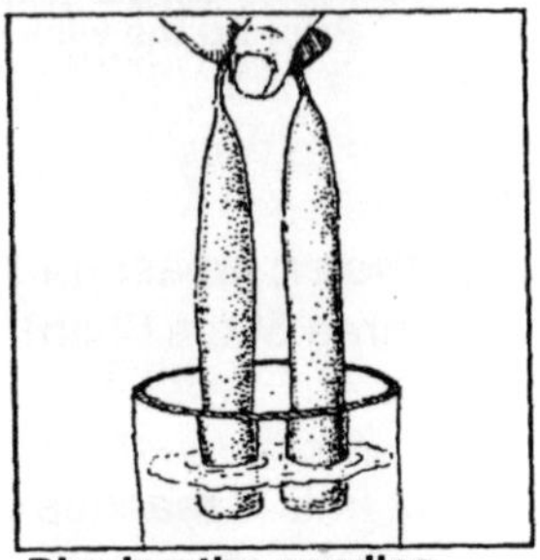

Dipping the candles.

METHOD

1. Put the chunks of wax into the dipping can, then stand the can in a saucepan half full of water. Heat the water until the wax melts and the temperature reaches 71°C (160°F), and then turn the heat right down. Remember to measure the temperature of the liquid wax, not the water. If you are not using wicks that you have already prepared, then prime them now.
2. Add the red dye to the wax until you achieve a good colour. Be careful not to use too much.
3. Check that the temperature of the wax is still 71°C (160°F), then dip each pair of wicks into the wax for about three seconds, and allow them to cool for one to four minutes depending upon the room temperature.
4. Repeat this process until the candles are the desired thickness.
5. Switch up the heat and raise the temperature of the wax to 82°C (180°F).
6. Give each pair of candles a final three-second dip, and allow them to cool for about three minutes. This final coating in hotter wax gives the candles a lovely smooth finish.
7. Trim the bases flat with a knife, taking care not to spoil the smooth finish with fingerprints. Allow the candles to cool for one hour. If you find that dipping produces a lumpy surface, then it means that your wax is too cold, so re-heat it to the correct temperature. Whilst

the candles are still soft, roll them against a work surface to flatten the lumps before dipping them again.

More about dipping

Home-made dipped candles are extremely attractive and have a special quality that factory-made candles just cannot match. There may be occasions when you want to produce dipped candles in quantity, e.g. to decorate the tables at a wedding feast, or to give as presents. Dipping them in pairs can be a laborious task, and with a little more preparation multiple dipping can speed up the process considerably.

Candles can be dipped in quantity by tying pairs of wicks to a frame. The only restriction on numbers is the diameter of the dipping can that you have available. The frame can be a simple rod, a hoop, or a square. Metal baking grids are especially useful to the home dipper. There are two important points to remember. Firstly, when tying the wicks on, make sure that you leave enough room between them to accommodate the finished candles – three candle diameters between wicks is about right. Secondly, do not forget that a frame of completed candles is a lot heavier than a frame of wicks.

Overdipping

Dramatic effects can be obtained by overdipping completed candles with wax of a strongly contrasting colour. The contrast is only revealed when the candle is lit.

How to – overdipping (blue on white)

EQUIPMENT AND MATERIALS

Large saucepan; thermometer; dipping can; some white dipped candles; 2kg (4lb 6oz) paraffin wax; 40g (approx. 2 discs) blue dye.

METHOD

1. Heat the wax in the dipping can to 82°C (180°F) and add dye to make a strong blue colour.
2. Dip the candles into the wax two or three times, leaving about thirty seconds between dips. If your candles do not pick up much colour, then your wax is too hot. If the coloured coating is scaly, then your wax is too hot. If the coloured coating is scaly, then your wax is too cold. In both cases, check and adjust the temperature before continuing.

Hand finishing

Freshly dipped candles can be worked by hand whilst they are still warm and soft. You can test if they are soft enough – the candle should bend easily into an S shape. If they have become too hard, then candles can be softened by dipping them into wax at 71°C (160°F) for about three seconds. You must then wait thirty seconds for the surface to cool before starting work. Wax will not stick to water, so when handling warm wax it helps to keep your hands, rolling-pin, work surface, etc., wet.

Plaited candles are very attractive, but do not use candles to teach yourself to plait. If you are not sure, then practise with bits of string. Even so, plaiting is often much easier with two people.

How to – plaited candles

Equipment and Materials

Scissors; a hook at a convenient working height; two pairs of freshly made candles about 1.25cm (½in) in diameter and at least 25cm (10in) long.

Method

1. Separate and discard one candle.
2. Hang the remaining pair over the hook and tie on the wick of the third candle, so that the tops of all three candles are at the same level.
3. Plait the candles together.
4. Squeeze the bottom ends together smoothly, and flatten the base so that the candle can stand up. Hang it up and allow it to cool for one hour.

The candle that was discarded from the plaiting process can be finished in a different way – by twisting. However, first of all, its diameter must be increased by further dipping.

Plating the candle.

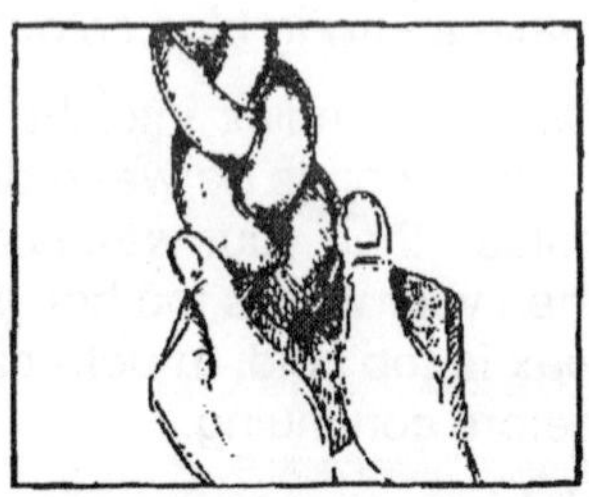

Squeezing the bottom ends of the candles together.

How to – twisted candles

Equipment and Materials

Rolling-pin and flat rolling surface; knife; one freshly dipped candle 25cm (10in) long and 2.5cm (1in) in diameter.

Method

1. Roll out the upper part of the candle until it is about 6mm (¼in) thick. Leave the bottom 2.5cm (1in) unrolled so that it can fit into a candle holder. If the candle cracks whilst rolling, then it has become too hard. Soften it by dipping it for three seconds at 71°C (160°F) and then waiting for thirty seconds.
2. Hold the candle upside-down, with the unrolled base in one hand and the flattened part nearest the base between the thumb and forefinger of your other hand.
3. Pull the candle slowly upwards, sliding it between your thumb and forefinger and turning it steadily.
4. Repeat the process to give a more exaggerated twist.
5. Trim the base flat and allow the candle to cool for one hour.

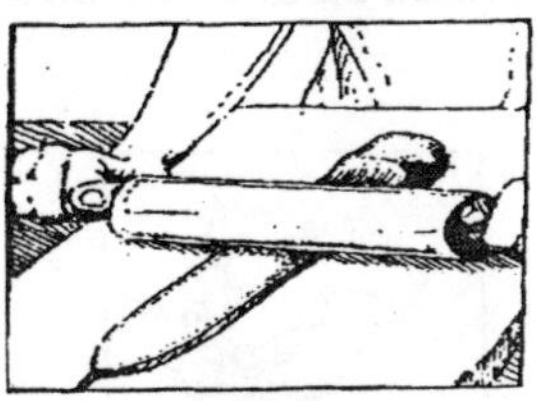

Flattening the candle.

Twisting the candle

Rolling

Simple candles can be made by rolling a sheet of wax around a prepared wick. The method of making a wax sheet that follows is particularly useful and should spark off many new ideas. It uses a large quantity of wax because of the height of the candles, but you can experiment with lesser quantities by using a smaller plywood template.

If, at any stage, the wax becomes too cold to work easily, then you can warm it gently with a hair dryer.

How to – flared spiral candles

Equipment and Materials

Double boiler; thermometer; triangular template (piece of plywood with sanded edges) 27 x 10 x 29cm (10¾ x 4 x 11½in) with wire attached to one corner to hold whilst dipping; two tall dipping cans; bowl of water; 10 kg (221b) dip and carve wax (paraffin wax will do if necessary); 100g (approx. 5 discs) pink dye; 30g (approx, 1½ discs chalky white dye; 200g (approx. 10 discs) black dye; two 30cm (12in) lengths of 1.25cm (½in) wick.

METHOD

1. Soak the plywood template in water for thirty minutes.
2. Heat 5kg (11lb) of wax to 71°C (160°F), prime the wicks, then add the pink and chalky white dyes.
3. Heat the other 5kg (11lb) of wax to the same temperature and add the black dye. (To get the dyes to disperse fully, it may be necessary to heat the wax to a higher temperature, and then allow it to cool for dipping.)
4. Remove the template from the water and shake off any excess drops.
5. Dip the template in the pink wax and wait for one minute. Repeat this five times more. Then, do the same with the black wax.
6. Wait until the wax is rubbery, then peel the wax from each face of the template.
7. Place one of the wax triangles pink side up and turn back the longest edge.

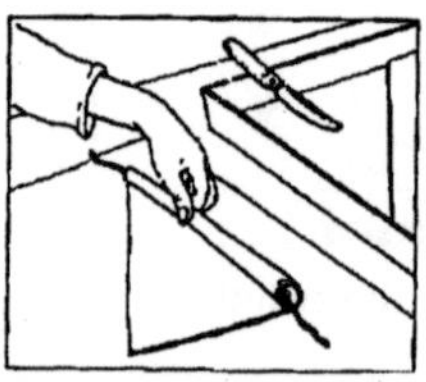

Rooling the wax into a tube.

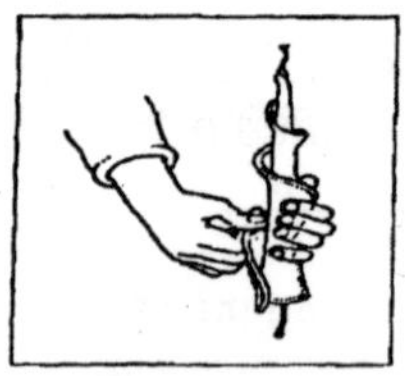

Smoothing the exposed edge into a spriral fin

8. Lay the wick along the longest side, about 1.25cm (½in) from the edge.
9. Fold the edge of the wax over the wick, and then roll it into a tube. Turn up the exposed edge with your fingers and smooth it into a spiral fin.
10. Flatten the base against your work surface and allow the candle to cool. Repeat with the other half of the wax.

Beeswax sheets

With one particular variety of wax, the technique of rolling really comes into its own. Beeswax is available in preformed honeycomb sheets, usually

34 x 20cm (13½ x 8in) in size. The sheets come in a variety of natural colours, ranging from creamy white to a rich medium brown, and dyed red and green. Beeswax sheets are workable at normal room temperature, although in cold weather they may need to be held near a heater for a few minutes until they soften.

Rolled beeswax candles can be very simple, or quite complicated – the choice is entirely yours. Candles can be straight or tapered, and sheets of contrasting natural shades can be rolled together for added effect. The sheets may also be cut into strips, which can be woven or wrapped around the outside of the candle.

How to – tapered beeswax candles

Equipment and Materials

Knife; metre (yard) rule; scissors; beeswax sheet 34 x 20cm (13½ x 8in); two 28cm (11in) lengths of 1.25cm (½in) wick.

Method

1. Cut the sheet in two across the diagonal.
2. Take one of the pieces and lay a wick along the shortest side of the triangle. The extra length of wick should project beyond the point.
3. Fold the edge of the sheet over the wick and roll the candle. Take care to produce a flat base.
4. Secure the loose end of the sheet by pressing it into the side of the candle.
5. Trim the wick to about 1.25cm (½in). Pinch a small piece of wax from the under-side of the base and squeeze it into the projecting wick. This ensures that the candle is ready to light.
6. Repeat the process with the other piece of beeswax sheet, but lay it the other way round. The finished candles will then be mirror images of each other.

Hand modelling

Wax is a very versatile material, and there is no limit to what creativity and imagination can achieve. With just a little skill and preparation, an ordinary dipped candle can be transformed into a realistic piece of wax sculpture – and a really exciting candle.

The instructions in this section are a little more complicated than the ones that you have been following until now, so read each sequence through carefully before you begin. If there is anything that you are not sure of, then refer back to the previous pages.

Perfumed wax flowers

Scented candles are a colourful and effective alternative to 'room deodorants', and they can also be used to provide that extra touch of atmosphere. By modelling flowers from scented wax, you can make a stunning perfumed centre-piece for a special dinner-table.

How to – floating roses

EQUIPMENT AND MATERIALS

Double boiler; thermometer; grease-proof paper; smooth-edged pastry cutter, or palette knife; wax glue; 1kg (2lb 3oz) dip and carve wax; eight 5cm (2in) lengths of 1.25cm (½in) wick; rose-scented wax perfume; wax pigment. These materials are sufficient to make eight floating rose candles.

METHOD

1. Melt the wax, heat it to 71°C (160°F), and prime the wicks.
2. Lay out some sheets of grease-proof paper. Switch off the heat, and add twelve drops of perfume to the wax.
3. Carefully pour out the wax on to the paper so that it forms layers about 3mm (⅛ in) thick, and allow it to cool until it is rubbery.
4. Cut petal shapes with the pastry cutter or palette knife. You will need petals of different sizes. Curve them with your fingers.
5. Squeeze two small petals around a wick and build up a rose flower by gluing on larger petals. Work quickly and make only one of two flowers at once. Wax that has cooled too much and become brittle can be softened with a hair dryer.
6. When your roses have cooled down completely, they can be painted with wax pigment.

All candles will float, but these ones will float upright. Placed in clear glass bowls and lit, they make a novel alternative to traditional forms of candle-light.

Wax fungi

Fly agaric is one of the many fungi found in fields and hedgerows. Incidentally, it is extremely poisonous, so do not be tempted to eat the real thing. Other fungi have equally distinctive shapes and colouring, and by modifying the basic technique a whole botanical garden of colourful fungi can be created.

How to – fly agaric toadstool

EQUIPMENT AND MATERIALS

Double boiler; thermometer; dipping can; wicking needle; one 25cm (10in) freshly made dipped candle about 2.5cm (1in) in diameter; paraffin wax initially at 71°C (160°F) – the quantity will depend upon the size of your dipping can; 250g (9oz) bright red overdipping wax; egg-cupful of undyed overdipping wax.

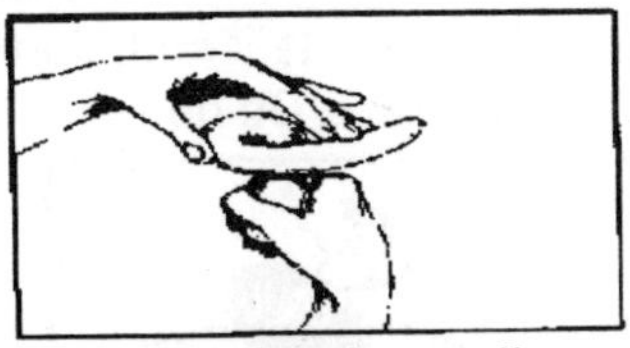

Bending the candle.

METHOD

1. Hold the candle in one hand, and with the other pull the wick straight out of the end of the candle. Put it aside for later use.

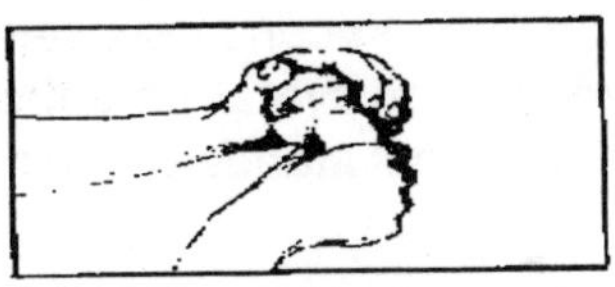

Smoothing the cap.

2. Bend the candle just below the midpoint, and wrap the upper part around to form the basis for the toadstool's cap. Shape the stalk, flaring it slightly at the base.

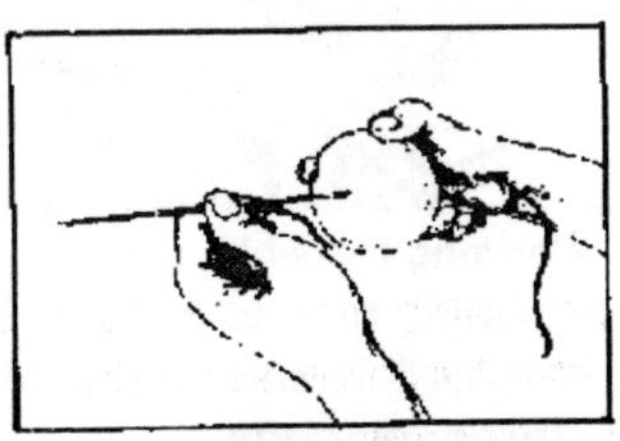

Re-threading the wick.

3. Hold the stalk and turn the cap against the palm of your hand to form a smooth rounded shape. To keep it soft, frequently re-dip the candle into the paraffin wax. Allow it to cool for thirty seconds after each dip.

Dipping the whole candle.

4. Use the wicking needle to re-thread the wick up through the stalk. Tie a knot in the wick at the stalk end, then pull the wick up so that the knot embeds in the base. Do not trim the other end of the wick.

Dipping the cap in red wax.

5. Heat the paraffin wax to 82°C (180°F), then re-dip the entire candle, stalk end first. Tow three-second dips, separated by a one minute cooling period, will give an overall smooth appearance. Flatten the base so that the toadstool stands up, and allow it to cool for thirty minutes.

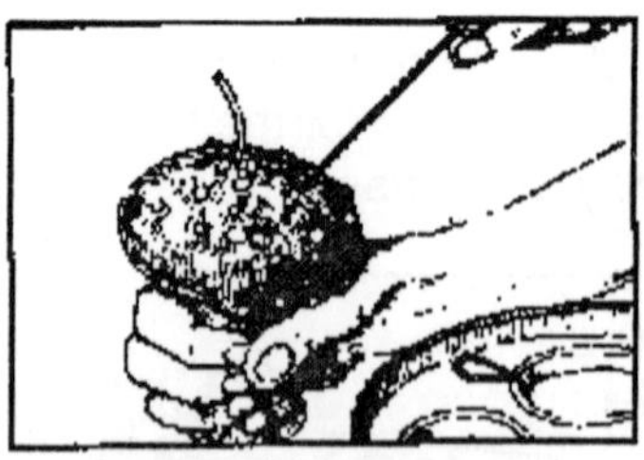

Forming the white spots.

6. Heat the red overdipping wax to 82°C (180°F) and dip the upper side of the cap into it for three seconds. After thirty seconds, dip it again for another three seconds.

7. Dip the sharp end of the wicking needle into the undyed overdipping wax at 82°C (180°F) and hold it there for about fifteen seconds. Then, place the point on the toadstool's cap, allowing the wax to run off and form a raised white dot. Repeat this to give a natural appearance, then allow the candle to cool fully for one hour.

5

CANDLE MAKING PROCESSES

There are a 4 methods producing candles on a small scale. These are outlined briefly as under and then described in detail later.

The Dipping Process : This technique involves immerising the candle wick in molten wax then withdrawing it, so that picks up wax as it emerges. The wax is allowed to cool and the process is repeated until the desired thickness has been built up. The equipment is very simple in principle and can also be easily made.

The Pouring Process : This technique involves suspending a wick in a container of molten wax and pouring hot wax wich drips back into the main container and can be used again. In terms of equipment this is simplest process. To produce candles of good quality in this way a fair degree of skill must be acquired.

The Moulding or Casting Process : The moulding process consists of filling a mould, in which a wick has been positioned, with molten, allowinig the wax to cool and then removing the completed candle from the mould. Except for very small outputs per day this is generally the adopted process. There is a certain degree of sophistication in mould design and fairly large number of moulds are needed. Equipment and accessories for casting candles in large numbers are avialable,and as they do not require electric power for operation, a description of them is included.

The Drawing Process : A long length of wick is passed back and forth horizontal through a bath of wax thereby forming a candle 'rope, which is accomadated on large drums which are manually oprerated. The 'rope' is then cut into standard candle lengths. A mechanised version of this machinery does give higher output, but at a higher capital cost.

Equipment : The equipment and accessories used for each of these four techniques and the processing methods are described in the following sections. Production rate is not affected by detail of equipment design. It is largely dependent upon a number of factors such as number of moulds or dipping points etc. This is because the factor is the colling rate of the candle, and except in elaborete water-cooled machines which make a large quantity of candles this is fixed for particular conditions.

The Dipping Process

Candle dipping offers a convenient methods of producing several hundred candles a day with relatively simple equipment. The candles may be 30cm long or even more in which case they can be cut as described in the section on the drawing process. Diameter of such candles can be up to 10 cm or even more.

A number of wicks ar e suspended and repeatedly dipped into wax to form by building up successive layers round the wicks. The excess wax drains off, but some remains at the lower end, which is therefore thicker, for this reason candles made in this way are often called tapered candles. However, with correct dipping technique and by discarding the lower 10 cm or so, candles of uniform diameter can be produced.

The equipment for dipping can range from an ordinary stick from which the wicks are suspended to elaborate commerciall-made machine (by Arthur Weissbach Fulda, W.Germany).

To obtain a well formed candles, the candle wick should be submerged in the molten wax and withdrawn as slowly as possible, so that the wax deposits are in even layers with no drips or surface imperfections.

Using this technique a semi-refined paraffin wax with a melting point of 54°C (130°F) is prepared first. To this 20 per cent of stearic acid is added. The addition of about 5 per cent bees wax if added will improve the qualities of adhesion of the wax. Micro-crystalline wax is not used as this tends to deposit at a faster rate than other waxes and prevents adhesion from occurring naturally

The paraffin wax is broken into pieces of a convenient size, weighed to the required quantity and placed in the vat (container). The right quantity of stearic acid or stearine, and the bees wax, if required is added to it. Gentle heating is done till all the contents have melted and blended together. When this occurs the blend is cooled to about 49°C (120°F) before attempting to dip. It is advisable to experiment with various temperatures to find out the one which suits the blend best. It is important that a sufficient quantity and depth of molten wax is maintained in the container at all times. Figure (1) illustrates a single dipping jig for dipping of 12 wicks at a time. Figure (2) illustrates a continuous dipping process using 4 or more wickholders suspended from a wheel. The production rates from this obviously much greater.

Approximate dimensions : Drawings not to scale.

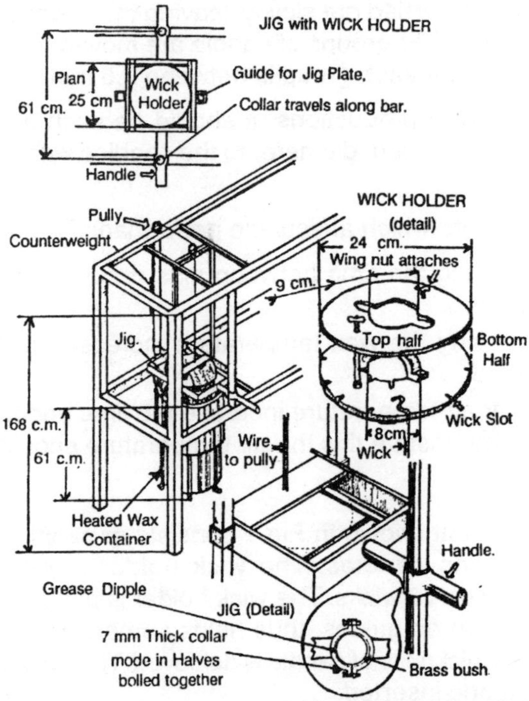

Figure 1.Simple Stand and Boiler for Dipping Process

A can or wax-pot which is deeper than the length of the longest candle to be made, is required.It should have sufficient height of the wax level to allow for displacement of the wax. It is heated by any one of the several methods described later, but as the wax is to be kept at a constant temperature for a considerable time and is cooled by immersion of candles, continuous heating, insulation and ideally thermostic controls are neccssary and advantageous.

The wax contains 90 per cent paraffin with a melting point of 58°C and 10 per cent stearine. Wicks for candles up to 3 cm diameter are 15 ply braided.

The wicks are tied to the dipping frames and a weight is hung at their lower ends. The wax is heated to 75° and the first group of wicks lowered into it.They are left to soak for 3 minutes to allow air and moisture to escape. This is done with each new group of wicks.The pre-waxed wicks are drawn through the fingers as they cool, to smooth off any lumps. This ensures that the final candles are smooth and uniform.

When all the wicks have been prewaxed, the properly dipping process begins. Each dip is carried out slowly, leaving the candle immersed in wax for 5 to 10 seconds. The groups of candle are moved round in turn and the time between dips for each group is between 2.5 minutes.

For commercial productions, it should be such as to give the best appearance and maximum diameter to the candles with the last number of dips

Various factors which affects the performance are as under.

(a) Increasing the time between dips reduces the number of dips needed.

(b) Increasing the wax temperature increases the number of dips needed.

(c) Higher air temperature increase the time needed between dips. To compenstate this the air temperature should be reduced.

Dipping

This equipment shown in Fig.1 consists of simple stand and boiler suitable for dipping candles. The wick holder is made of wood and approximately holds 12 wicks. The wick holder is placed in a jig in which it slides up and down on guides, thus holds immersing the wick each time until the required thickness of candle is achieved. The holder is then removed and the second one inserted.

The equipment shown in Fig. 2 consists of a continuous dipping process with four or more wick holders. The production rate from this machine is obviously much greater than that from the single wick holder shown in Fig. 1.

Finally, the candels are removed, trimmed at their lower ends to remove the excess wax & to maintain a uniform diameter and allowed to cool. They may be rolled in the same way as in the case of poured candles. An alternative and convenient method of removing the weights is to dip the ends in molten wax, and then cutting the wicks along with the weights.

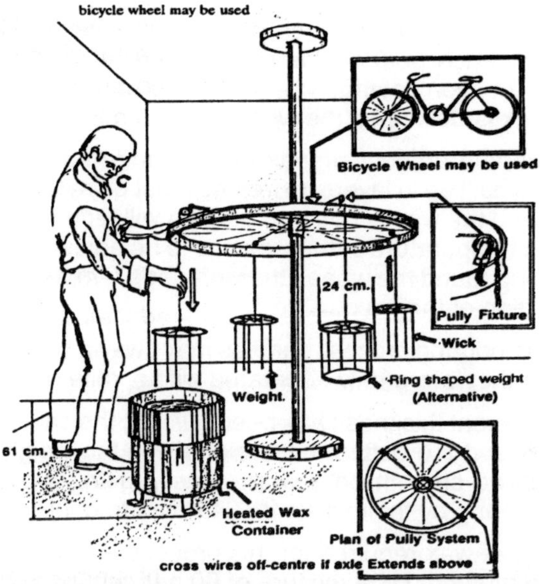

Approximate dimensions : Drawings not to scale.

Figure 2. Continous Dipping Process for Candles Making

Equipment Required

Scales	for weighing the various materials
Thermometer	for checking the wax temperature
Sharp knife	for trimming the ends of finished candles
Scissors	for cutting the wicks
Small weights	for keeping the wicks vertical and taut (lead preferred)
Boiler or vat	for melting the wax-must be of seamless construction
Storage rack	for storing the candles between dipping operation
Wick holders	required for dipping operations and also for the operation (jigs) or candle hangers
Wood boards	for making shelves and working surfaces
Wheel	for incorporating a continuous dipping process
Smooth slab	for rolling the ends of candles. These should be preferably made of marble, but glass or metal can also be used

The Pouring Process

The wax is heated to a temperature of 75° C and by using the ladle the wax is poured down on each wick in turn, the wax then falls off the wicks and goes back into the melter. It is possible to make the excess wax of all into a separate can. As each pouring is made the wheel is slightly rotated. During each pouring the wick should be twisted slowly, which helped to form an even coatng. The process is continued until the desired thickness of wax is built upon the wicks.

Only a certain amount of wax can be added at each pouring and since the wax is built up in layers, extremes must be avoided. If the candles are too warm and the wax is hot, one pouring will tend to melt the previous one off. So, the temperature of the wax has to be adjusted according to the speed of working round the wheel, the workshop temperature and also the exact composition of the wax.

During the pouring process candles may sway a bit and stick together. If this happens they are gently separated with a knife or by tapping.

When sufficient thickness has been built up, the candles are removed from the wheel and the bottom ends along with the weights cut off. They can then be rolled smooth on a warm glass, metal or stone slab, after which they are hung by their wicks for 24 hours to cool.

The blend of wax required for this process is the same as that used for the dipping method, i.e. a mixture of 90 per cent paraffin wax of (58°C melting point) and 10 per cent stearine. For making candles for churches a proportion of beewax is generally added, although this considerablly increase the cost.

Approximate dimensions: Drawing not to scale

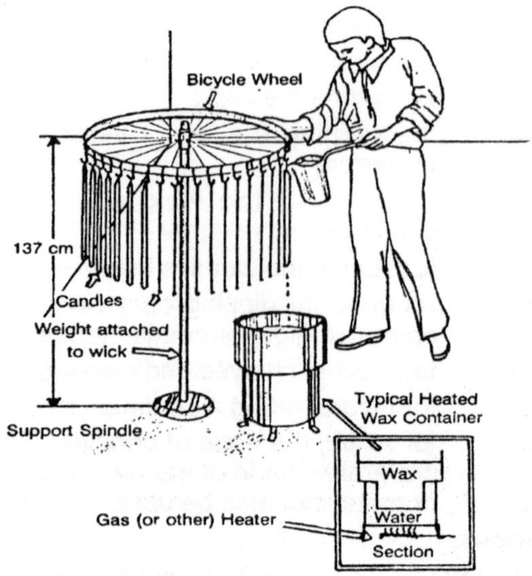

Figure 3. Pouring Process for Candles Making

This rig consists of a rim of an old cycle wheel in a horizontal plane by a vertical shaft, the length of which is determined, supported by a suitable working position. The bottom ends of the shaft should be fixed on a heavy base-plate, so that the whole construction is safe for working, the wheel should be able to rotate freely, Small metal hooks made from approximately 3 mm diameter wire are fixed to the outer rim of the wheel, from which the wicks are suspended and kept rigid in a vertical position using a small lead weight at the bottom of each wick. A heated container similar to that used in the previous technique, is positioned so that the outer rim of the wheel is just above the centre of the container. A small ladle is required for pouring the molten wax over the wick.

The Moulding or Casting Process

Casting (or moulding) is most suitable under the following conditions

For a household making candles only for its own consumption and also when it is very small.

For candles which are used as decorative items rather than strictly for the utility, in which many techniques of colouring, texturing items and the production of special shapes are used, and for candles over 4 cm in diameter.

For mass production of ordinary candles, special machines are used.

Thus casting is not really suitable for use on a small scale industry basis. The technical reasons are that moulds must be really well designed and accurately made if they are to be reliable and continual attention during cooling is needed for topping up as the wax contracts and that for a comparable output to, say candle-drawing, a large number of moulds are needed. However this method can produce highly finished and decorative candles.

The technique is very simple. It consists of suspending a wick in a mould and tied to a rod at the top and also fixed at the bottom with a knot and then filling the cavity of the mould with molten wax. When the wax has cooled and set, the finished candle can be removed from the mould and this will be an exact replica of the inside shape of the mould. One advantage of using this method is that it does not require much work to be done. Once the candle is removed from the mould. The wax in the mould must be cooled slowly. As the wax is cools it shrinks, so a little more wax is added very often, just to keep the top more or less level. When the candle has completely set, it comes out of the mould without any trouble. If the candle does tend to bind in the mould it is likely that the wax and temperature used are not correct for this method.

A hard wax is normally used for casting as it is less likely to adhere to the mould.As hardness can be gauged by high melting point,wax which melts in the region of 68°C (140°F-155°F) generally used. The temperature for filling a mould should not be less than 80°C (175°F) and not higher than 88°C (190°F).

A good basic paraffin wax should be selected for the moulding. It should be hard and posses a high melting point at the temperature previously mentioned. A relatively high percentage of stearic acid, between 10 and 30 per cent is generally added and to obtain a good surface finish resistant to abrasion and dust pene-tration, 3 per cent of micro-crystalline wax is necessary. This will also ensure a good clean release from the mould, as it is very hard to adhere. This blend will produce a good quality, long burning candle.

A perfectly adequate simple candle can be made by using only paraffin wax, which could be sufficient, depending upon the market demand. As the wax in the mould cools down,each candle should be probed with a long thin rod and opened. If any hole is seen, this should be filled with fresh wax. The process may have to be repeated until all the wax has solidified and hardened.During solidification, 20 per cent and so, if this procedure is not followed there likely to be holes in the candles, particularly in the region of the wick.

Once, the wax has become solid,but not yet cooled down solid, the mould is immersed in water, if it is put in running water, cooling is much faster.When the wax has cooled down the wicks are taken off the top metal bar (s) and the candles are pushed out of the moulds pressing the bottom plugs or bungs through.

If there are persistent problems of release,following can be tried:

The proportion of stearine should increased.

The inside of the mould tubes should be tin plated and moulds should be sprayed with silicon(expensive).

Equipment Required

Weighing scales
Thermometer
Pair of scissors
Small weights (lead is best)
Boiler or vat or heating vessel
Small ladle
Bench or Table
Candle moulds

Moulding

The illustration shows a bench,boiler and moulds required for this process. Only rough dimensions are shown on these sketches because it is felt that these requirements are best left to those who are able to asses the most suitable size of bench and moulds together with the number that meets their own individual output requirements. A simple design of a set moulds is shown.

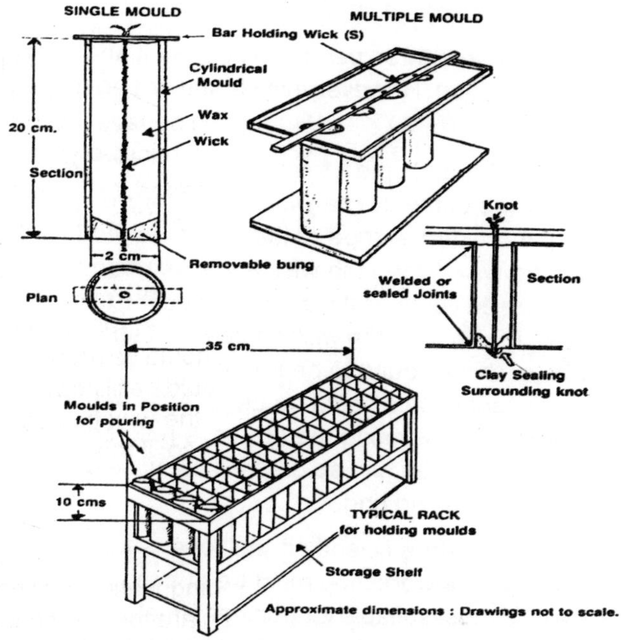

Figure 4.Moulding Process for Candle Making

The bench may be of wood construction, but it is suggested that the main surface should be covered with a thin metal sheet. This ensures easier cleaning of any surplus wax that may overflow from the moulds while pouring. The top section of the bench is divided into small square boxes to ensure that the moulds remain in an upright steady position thus avoiding, any accidental overturning of the moulds while the pouring action in progress. The position of the wax boiler should be located in a convenient position to ensure easy access to the wax.

The mould is made from a metal seamless pipe but any suitable container can be used provided the inside is smooth and parallel, thus ensuring easy removal of the candle when completed. The metal bung at base of the mould gives a suitable shape to the top of the finished candle but it also can be pushed in an upward direction, thus facilitating the removal of the finished candle without damage. The small metal bar at the top of the mould is used for supporting the candle wick.

The Candle Drawing Method

This method is adopted when a large number of candles are required to be produced. This method requires a simple machine which can be made by any craftsman, with this machine candles upto 6 cm diameter can be made but 3 cm is a more practical limit

This method requires three people to operate it and some skill has to be developed for operation. However this should not be present a serious problem.

The wax used is heated upto a temperature of 75°C. The wax contains a ten per cent stearine content. The wicks used for the candle upto 3 cm diameter are 15 ply braided. A rope of the candle is produced by drawing the wick through the wax. When the wick is passed through the trough for the first time it is passed very slowly and care must be taken to ensure that all air escapes from the wick. As the wick comes out it should be smoothened within the fingers, or this is found to be uncomfortable, a piece of thick felt or any other convenient device could be used. After the first pass through the trough the direction of winding the drums is reversed so that the wick picks up another layer of wax and so on untill the waxed rope is exactly of the same as that of the sizing ring.

This machine will run efficiently if the rope is kept warm enough to remain flexible so that the workshop must be at a temperature of the least 25°C. This process is most suitable for tropical climates. In cooler or tropical climates. In cooler areas the work shop must be heated and maintained at a temperature of at least 30°C.

When the rope is complete it must be cut into the required size of candle lengths,specific cutting machines are also available for this. However the job can also be done manually, the candle rope is led on to a cutting table of any smooth and hard material and cut into the desired length with a sharp knife. This is not difficult while the wax is fairly soft enough. After this, about 1cm of must be exposed at one end of each candle. Using knife the wax can be cut with a rolling rather than a downward cutting action without at the same time cutting the wick and the butt of the wax is removed. The technique is soon picked up and in actual practice the cutting to length and exposing the wick are done at the same time. Sometimes the cutting is done in such a manner that the ends of the candles are tapered. This is done by hand by rolling the end of the candle at an angle on a hard surface. However this is not necessary for manufacture these candles for utility purpose though the appearance of the candles is greatly unproved.

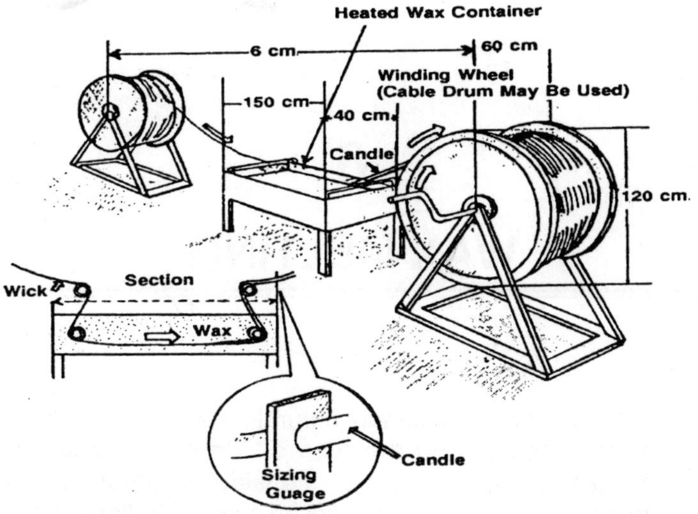

Approximate dimensions : Drawing not to scale

Figure 5. Drawing Process for Candle Making

Drawing

The wick is first wound on a large drum of about 120 cm.diameter and 60 cm wide.This is mounted on horizontal scale and fitted with a handle for turning.The wick is then passed through a heated trough containig wax. The trough is generally 150 cms long and 40 cms wide and 14 cms deep.At the end of the trough is a sizing gauge which is a ring of steel or (any hard wood) with a series of varying sized holes drilled through it. The wick passes through one of these holes which controls the finished size of the candles. Finally the work is led through the trough of molten wax to a second drum similar to the first.

6

WAX MELTING

Methods

All the methods of making candle naturally start with melting the wax. The equipment, ofcourse, on the type of fuel or the source of heat available.The saftey aspect must be considered before any working operation is designed.The wax should not be over heated as there is always the risk of fire due to the vapourising of the wax since the molten wax has a reasonably high flash point. However the wax should not be heated above 150°C which is a high temperature, many unpleasant and dangerous fumes are given if this temperature is well above that needed for making candles but the manufacturing workshop should always be well ventilated. It is but natural that any wax split into a naked flame or into a red-hot electric hearths will catch fire immediately, and a large scale fire is then very likely. So although these heaters can be used, precuations must be taken against this kind of accident.

Heating Equipment

Electricity : This is necessary for small medium size workshops, if available.Tanks melting pots can be placed on ceramic plate type heaters, or heating elements can be bolted to the bottom of a tank. Immersion heaters are at all costs to be avoided.

Gas tanks or pots placed on gas heaters can be used provided the bottom is thick enough to prevent burning the wax. Asbestos mats may used under the pot, but care has to be taken regularly for their resistance to heat and degradation.Thus,due to use,as their life span is not long.The precaution about naked flames,of course,applies here.

Small quantities of wax used in the pouring technique can be melted in a gas heated water jacket. Melting is rather slow but the wax will remain in molten state for a longer time. However care must be taken not to boil the water and as this is very likely to happen. Hence water jackets are not always considered ideal.

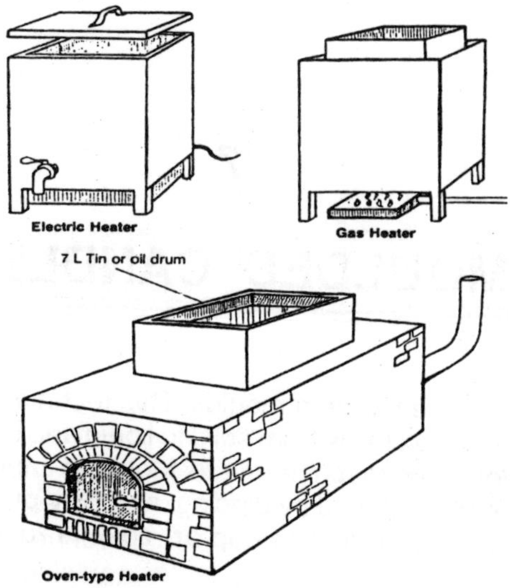

Figure 6. Heating Equipment for Melting Wax

Solid fuel : Where no other fuel is available,melting pots can be placed on specially constructed heating retorts or Bhattis. A simple Bhatti can be built from fire proof bricks.

Steam : In a large installations steam heating is used, the steam being led in jacketted heating pots. An attempt should not be made to construct steam heating plant unless proper engineering facilities are available.

For all the four methods, the wax pots and tanks should be leak proof (not soldered) and should be of steel,iron or aluminium. Copper and brass should be avoided as they are likely to cause oxidation.

Thermometers : It ispossible to make candles without using a thermometer but the operation tends to be hit or miss. Fortunately, thermometers are not very expensive several types are available in the market. In all cases a range from 100°C-150°C is needed.

Types available in the market include an ordinary mercury in glass, reading up to 100°C which is very cheap; secondly a sugar thermometer, normally used in household for botting, jam making etc.; thirdly a commercial rotary type all metal thermometer which tends to be rather more expensive, and lastly there is the remote dial or type thermometer,where the bulb is fixed into the tank and the dial mounted on a convienient bracket nearby such thermometer.

Wax containers can be of any suitable size provided they are leak proof and do not have soldered joints. They can be of iron steel or aluminium, and heated by electricity, gas or over simple heating retort or bhati.

7

MOULDED CANDLES

Most candles are made in moulds. This technique makes full use of the ease with which wax turns from solid to liquid and back again. However, moulded does not mean machine-made. Moulded candles are every bit as handmade as those produced by dipping, and they provide endless scope for exciting variations, from vivid pop art colours to subtle impressionist landscapes.

Candle moulds are available in a bewildering variety of shapes and sizes, but in all cases the basic technique is the same. A prepared wick is threaded through the mould, which is then filled with molten wax. The mould is cooled in a water bath and is periodically topped up with wax. When cold, the candle is removed and the wick is trimmed.

It sounds simple, and it is. However, I do urge you to read through the following three pages carefully, even if you have no intention of making a one-colour candle. Some of the candles in this section can take several hours to produce, and, because 'there's many a slip twixt cup and lip', a little patience and practice now might well save you heartache at the end of some future afternoon.

Moulds

All the candles in this section are based on easily available commercial moulds. However, for the more adventurous, there are some notes on improvising and making your own moulds. The basic types of mould are listed here.

Rigid plastic : Usually transparent, these are ideal for the beginner and are available in a variety of geometric shapes.

Glass : These moulds produce candles with a high gloss finish, but they are fragile and limited to cylindrical shapes.

Metal : These are sturdy and have excellent cooling properties.

Flexible PVC : These are ideal for irregular shapes, such as candle fruits, and give a good finish.

Rubber: These moulds produce candles with a matt finish. They tend to deteriorate with repeated use, but are ideal for high relief surfaces.

Most moulded candles start with a primed wick. If you have forgotten how to dip your wick, then go back to page 15 and refresh your memory.

How to – wicking up

EQUIPMENT AND MATERIALS

Cylindrical mould; wicking needle; bowl of water; mould seal; one primed wick.

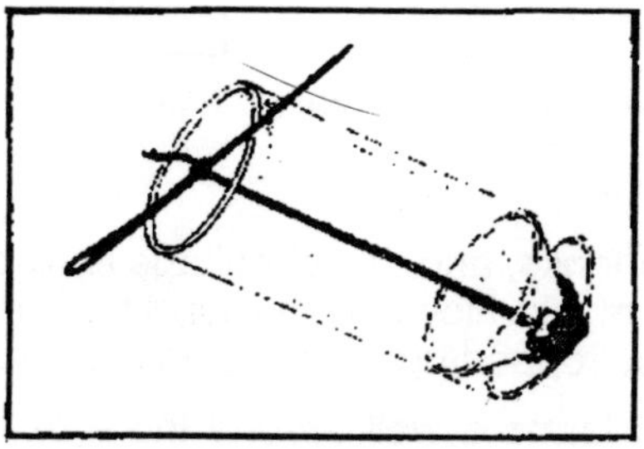

Discs of wax dye.

METHOD

1. Thread the primed wick up through the small hole in the end of the mould. The coated end should always be at the 'burning end' of the candle.
2. Place the wicking needle across the base of the mould and tie the wick to it.
3. Pull the other end of the wick tight and secure it with a lump of mould seal – this is reusable so do not be stingy.
4. Hold the sealed end of the mould under water to check that the mould seal is watertight.

Water baths

Wax poured into a mould takes a long time to cool. The cooling time can be shortened by using a water bath, that is, a bowl of cold water. Candles can be allowed to cool at room temperature, but water cooling improves appearance and gives smoother mould release.

Almost any large bowl can be used, provided that its base is level enough for the mould to stand upright and it is deep enough for the mould. Normally, a water bath is filled to within 1.25cm (½in) of the base of the inverted mould. An ideal temperature for water baths is 10–15°C (50–59°F); below 10°C (50°F) thermal shock may cause cracking. In midwinter it may be necessary to warm up water from the cold tap.

Wax floats, and so will a filled mould. Therefore, a weight (1kg/2lb) must be used to keep the mould stable. The technique of positioning the weight is worth practising, as toppling a freshly poured candle is not the right way to find out that your weight does not balance properly.

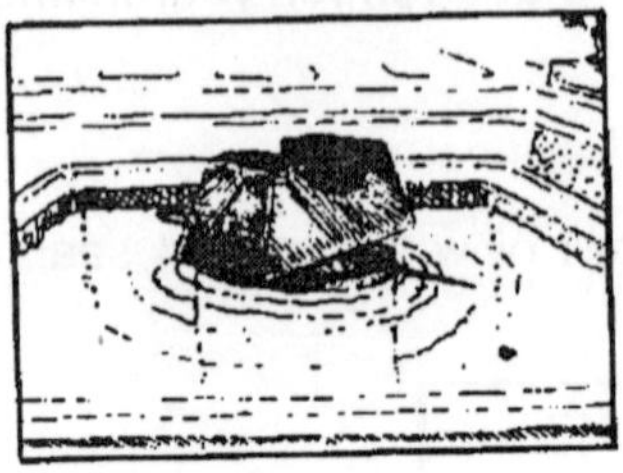

Weighting the mould in the water bath.

Topping up the mould with hot wax.

Topping up

As wax cools it shrinks, and this shrinkage is what enables a candle to be removed from its mould. However, not all of the shrinkage is desirable, and the candle must be topped up carefully as it cools.

The cooling wax forms a well around the wick area. This must be filled, but not overfilled, and it is very important that no hot wax spills over between the candle and the mould. If this occurs, then the candle will become very difficult to remove from the mould.

Successful topping up depends upon a steady hand and precise control over the amount of wax that you are delivering. It also helps to use a can or pan with a suitable spout, that is, one that is not too wide. To begin with, you may find it helpful to practise pouring small amounts of water into a narrow-necked bottle.

The secrets of a good moulded candle are correct pouring temperatures and knowing how to play the waiting game. Use the cooling time to good purpose, and do not let the clock oppress you. Whatever you do, if you want good results then learn to resist temptation. Do not fiddle or poke at the well until the first hour has passed, and once you have topped up the candle leave it alone – a watched candle never sets!

Waxes for moulding

Never make assumptions about waxes and moulds; always check the instructions thoroughly. With most rigid moulds, a quantity (usually 10 per cent) of stearin can be added to paraffin wax to increase the amount of shrinkage. But with some other moulds, such as rubber, the stearin rots the surface of the mould and must not be used.

Beeswax presents problems when used in moulds because it is so sticky. With rigid moulds, a release agent must always be applied to the inside of mould if more than 10 per cent beeswax is to be used.

ONE-COLOUR CANDLES

These are the simplest moulded candles and will provide you with valuable experience. All of the basic moulding techniques are employed, and once you have made one you can move on with confidence to more sophisticated candles.

The instructions are based on one of the most common types of commercial mould. If you use a different mould and are not sure about the quantity of wax, then fill the mould with water and measure it. Every 100cm³ (1/5pt) of water represents 90g (3¼oz) of cold wax.

Melting the stearin.

How to – one-colour candle

EQUIPMENT AND MATERIALS

Double boiler; saucepan; thermometer; cylindrical mould 20cm (8in) tall and 5cm (2in) in diameter; wicking needle; water bath; weight; scissors; 225g (8oz) paraffin wax; 25g (1oz) stearin; 2.5g (approx. 1/8 disc) red wax dye; 25cm (10in) length of 5cm (2in) wick; mould seal.

Adding the paraffin wax.

METHOD

1. Melt the stearin in the double boiler, and then add the dye.
2. When the dye has dissolved, add the paraffin wax.
3. Whilst the wax is melting, wick up the mould. Check that the mould seal is watertight. If it leaks, then dry the inside of the mould thoroughly before wicking up again.

Pouring the wax into the inverted mould.

4. Heat the wax to 93°C (199°F) and carefully pour it into the middle of the inverted mould, trying not to touch the sides. Do not fill the mould completely, but leave about 1.25cm (½in) at the end.

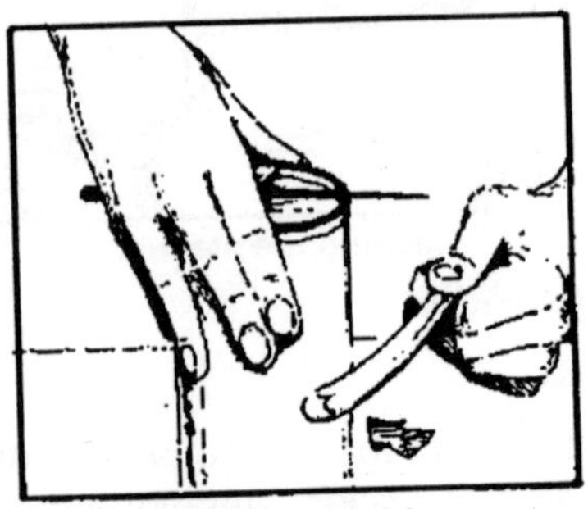

Tapping the mould.

5. Wait two minutes, then give the mould a sharp tap with the scissors or a spoon handle. This will shake loose any bubbles of air that are attached to the inside of the mould.

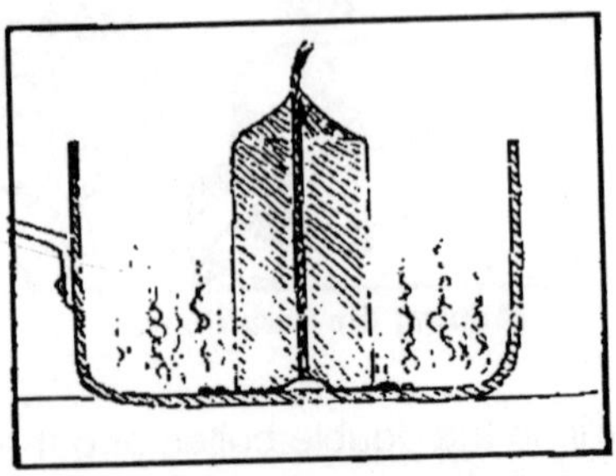

Levelling the base of the candle.

6. Stand the mould in the water bath using the weight to hold it down. The level of the water in the bath should be the same as the level of the wax in the mould. Allow it to cool for one hour.

7. A conical well will form around the wick. Remove the mould from the bath and prick the surface of the well with a wicking needle.
8. Re-heat the wax to 93°C (199°F) and carefully top up the well. Do not top up beyond the original level, as this will overfill the mould and make the candle difficult to extract.
9. Replace the mould in the water bath for a further hour until the candle has cooled down completely.
10. Take the mould out of the water and remove the mould seal. Turn the mould the right way up and your candle will slide out. With the scissors, trim the wick flush with the base, then use a warm pan to level the base so that the candle stands upright.

Multicoloured candles

Different coloured waxes can be used in the same candle to great effect. Bright, primary colours can be paired in eye-catching contrast. Alternatively, subtle, toning shades can produce a restful and evocative result. The choice is all yours.

Once you have mastered the techniques outlined on the following pages, there is no end to the potential for experiment. With practice, you will be able to transform a vision seen in the mind's eye into the physical reality of a beautiful candle.

Layered candles

Pouring alternate layers of contrasting wax produces a two-tone, banded candle. The layers can be as thick or as thin as you like, although layers less than 1.25cm (½in) thick are difficult to pour.

Another idea is to use just one colour, but start with a very pale shade and then add a little more dye each time you pour. The graduated tones of the finished candle will blend imperceptibly into each other.

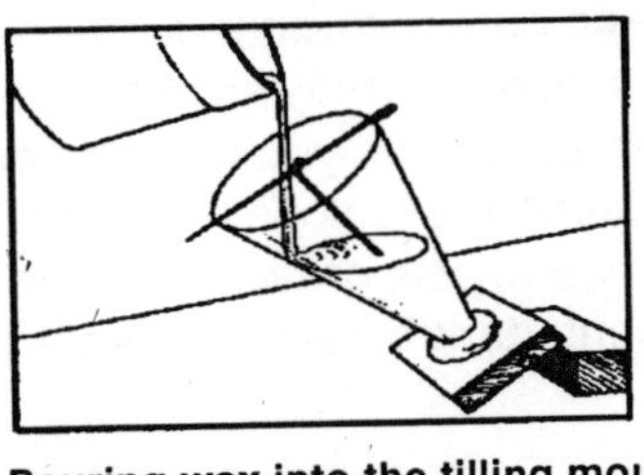

Pouring wax into the tilling mould.

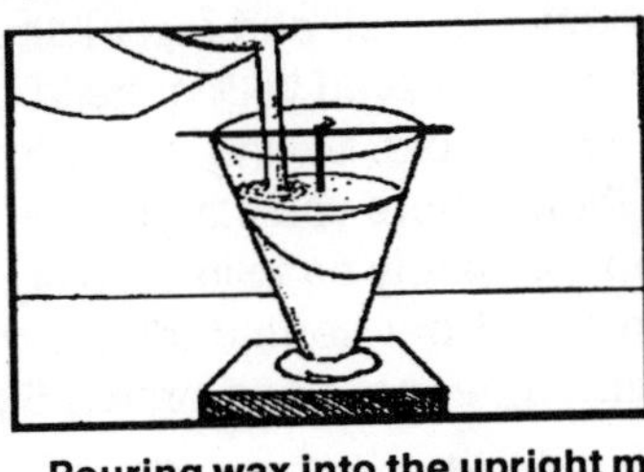

Pouring wax into the upright mould.

How to – angled layered candle

EQUIPMENT AND MATERIALS

Double boiler; thermometer; conical mould 12.5 cm (5in) high; tilting block; wicking needle; water bath; weigth; scissors; paper tissue; 165g (6oz) paraffin wax; 15g (½oz) stearin; red, green and yellow dyes; 17.5 cm (7in) length of 2.5 cm (1in) wick; mould sea.

METHOD

1. Wick up the mould.
2. Melt 55g (2oz) paraffin wax 5g ($\frac{1}{6}$ oz) stearin and add yellow dye. You will need a strong colour so use plenty of dye. Heat the wax to 93°C (199°F).
3. Place the mould on the tilting block and pour in the yellow wax. After one minute, tap the mould to release any air bubbles. Allow it to cool until the surface is rubbery and will break, not bend, when prodded.
4. Wipe out the double boiler with tissu and, using the same quantities, prepare the green wax and heat it to 82°C (180°F).
5. Tilt the mould to the other side and pour in the green wax. Tap out any air allow it to cool until the surface is rubbery.
6. Prepare the red wax and pour it into the upright mould at 82°C (180°F), making a level base. Tap out any air and then place it in the water bath to cool for half an hour. If necessary, then top up with red wax at 93°C (199°F).
7. Allow the candle to cool for a further hour, then remove it from the mould, trim the wick, and flatten the base.

Landscapes in wax

By combining the layering technique with a little simple sculpture, you can create a candle that contains a miniature landscape of a river, hills and mountains.

This candle involves five or six different colours, and you will probably find it easier to melt and mix all the separate colours beforehand. The best results are achieved with quite subtle colours, and wax only shows its true colour when cold. Mixing the colours beforehand allows you to judge and adjust them before you start pouring. The propertions of colour in this candle are approximately as follows: sky blue 40 per cent; pale green 10 per cent; mid-green 25 per cent; dark green 15 per cent; dark blue 10 per cent (or dark blue 5 per cent and brown 5 per cent).

How to – landscape candle

EQUIPMENT AND MATERIALS

Double boiler; thermometer; cylindrical mould 20cm (8in) tall and 5cm (2in) in diameter; wicking needle; teaspoon with rounded handle; matchstick;

water bath; weight; scissors; 225g (8oz) paraffin wax; 25g (1oz) stearin; blue, green, and brown (if required) dyes; 25cm (10in) length of 5cm (2in) wick; mould seal.

METHOD

1. Wick up the mould. Melt the paraffin wax and stearin, and mix up all of the colours in the proportions given above.
2. Heat the pale blue wax to 82°C (180°F) and pour it into the mould. Wait for one minute and tap out any air. Place it in the water bath to cool until the wax is set but still warm.
3. Remove it from the water and, using the teaspoon handle, carve out some pointed mountain peaks.
4. Heat the pale green wax to 82°C (180°F) and pour in into the mould. Tap out any air and allow it to cool until the wax is set but still warm.
5. Use the spoon to carve out the hills below the peaks. Heat the mid-green wax and pour it in. Allow it to set.
6. Now carve out some foothills, trying to make them overlap the hills. Pour in the dark green wax and allow it to cool.
7. With the matchstick, trace the course of the river down one of the overlapping valleys. The river should widen towards the base and make a lake. Pour in the dark blue wax to fill the river and lake. Allow it to cool.
8. The final thin layer can be either brown for soil, or more blue to create an island landscape.
9. After pouring all the layers, allow the finished candle to cool in the water bath for a further hour before removing it from the mould. Finally, trim the wick and flatten the base of the candle.

Swirling and chunks

Bright, cheerful candles can be made by pouring coloured wax over chunks of contrasting wax. This is a good way of using up 'failed' candles or any other odd bits of wax.

Star-shaped moulds are the best for chunk-laden candles because they provide the most opportunities to place chunks to good effect. Otherwise, the procedure is the same as for a one-colour candle.

An exciting refinement is to pour in plain wax and then spoon in dye so that it creats swirling patterns as it spreads. Doing this means using wax that is hotter than the boiling point of water, so the wax must be heated directly. Please be careful when doing this, as at these temperatures wax becomes flammable. Timing and temperature are critical with this type of candle. The wax must be but the dyes should only be warm. The secret is in putting the candle into the water bath before the swirls of colour lose definition.

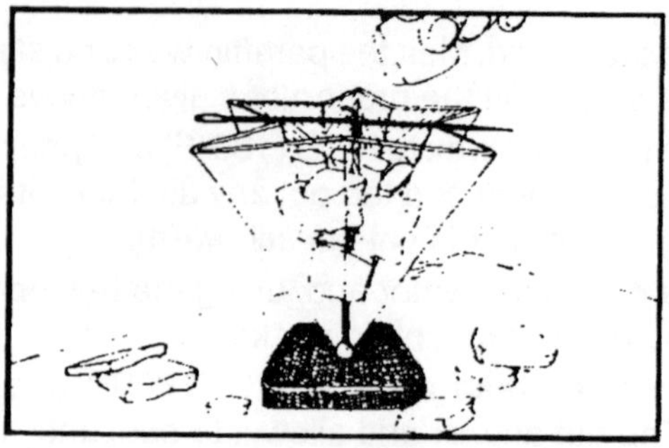

Placing wax chunks in the mould.

How to–swirly chunked candle

EQUIPMENT AND MATERIALS

Saucepan; egg poacher; thermometer; wicking needle; three teaspoons; water bath; weight; 60g (2oz) coloured wax poured out into a sheet about 7mm (¼in) thick and allowed to go cold; 90g (3¼oz) paraffin wax; 10g ($\frac{1}{3}$ oz) stearin; three pieces of dye in contrasting colours; star-shaped mould 15cm (6in) high; 20cm (8in) length of 2.5cm (1in) wick; mould seal.

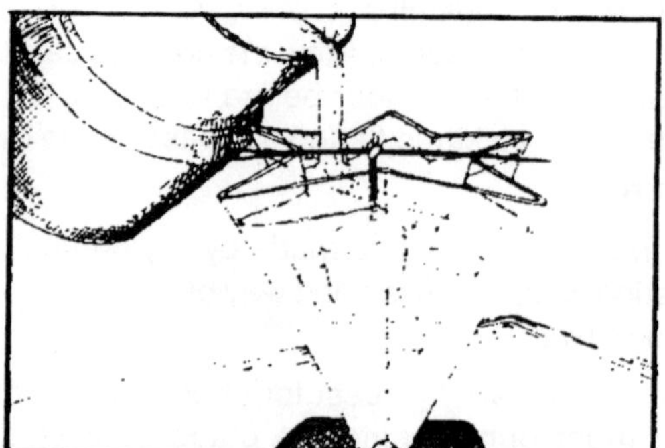

Pouring wax/stearin mixture into the mould.

METHOD

1. Wick up the mould. Break up the sheet of wax into 1–2cm (½–¾in) chunks and place them in the mould. Take care not to disturb or dislodge the wick.

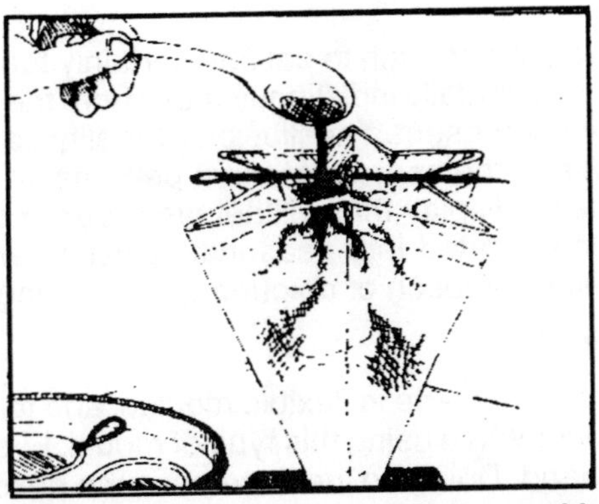

Spooning drops of melted dye into the mould.

2. Melt the dyes in the egg poacher–they should only just be liquid.
3. Melt the wax and stearin in the saucepan and heat to 127°C (260°F). Gently pour it into the centre of the mould, covering all of the chunks.

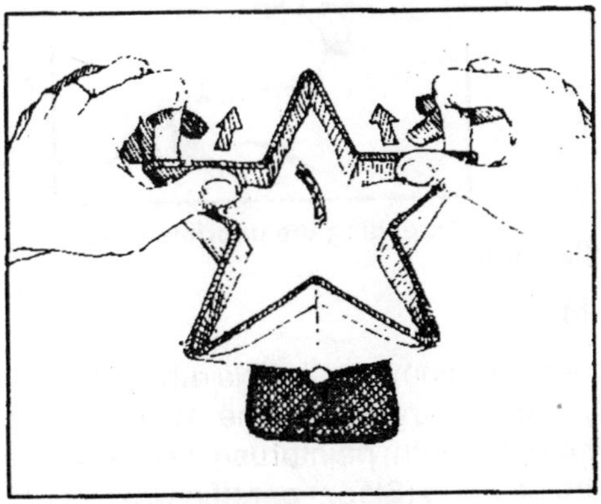

Releasing the candle.

4. Using a different spoon for each colour, spoon drops of dye into the mould. Allow about forty–five seconds for the dyes to swirl, them place the mould in a cold water bath and weight it. Allow it to cool for two hours.
5. Release your candle by gently pressing the sides of the mould outwards whilst supporting the points with your fingers.

Candle Fruits

These look good enough to eat and certainly too good to burn. A well-made candle fruit is virtually indistinguishable from the real thing and makes a wonderful novelty present. The illusion of reality can be enhanced even further by the use of the appropriate fruit perfume. In a bowl, candle fruits make an appetizing display that will not discolour or go mouldy. Individual fruits can be incorporated into seasonal flower arrangements, or simply placed on a shelf for a touch of colour and something to tease the eye.

Wicks and water bath

Candle fruits are made in flexible moulds, and there are two essential points to remember when using this type of mould. Firstly, you do not prime the wick beforehand. Doing so just increases the possibility of molten wax leaking out of the mould. When new, flexible moulds have no hole at the upper end, so you must make the hole with the wicking needle. Make it as small as you possibly can. Secondly, a suitable water bath needs to be selected for each mould. Large quantities of water will cause the mould to distort as it cools. For the best results, there should be no more than 5 cm (2in) of water between the mould and the sides of the water bath.

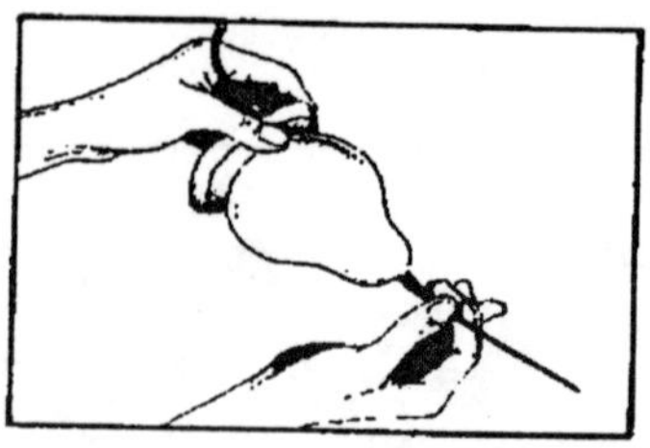

Threading the unprimed wick.

How to – candle pear

EQUIPMENT AND MATERIALS

Double boiler; thermometer; flexible rubber pear mould; wicking needle; water bath only slightly larger than the mould; stiff carboard template to support neck of mould; cloth; paintbrush; craft knife; dipping can; washing-up liquid; white spirit; 240g (8½oz) paraffin wax; 3g (1/7 disc) 'pear fruit' dye; 15cm (6in) length of 3.75cm (1½in) wick; burnt sienna poster paint; sufficient green or yellow wax (not too strong a colour) to dip the finished candle.

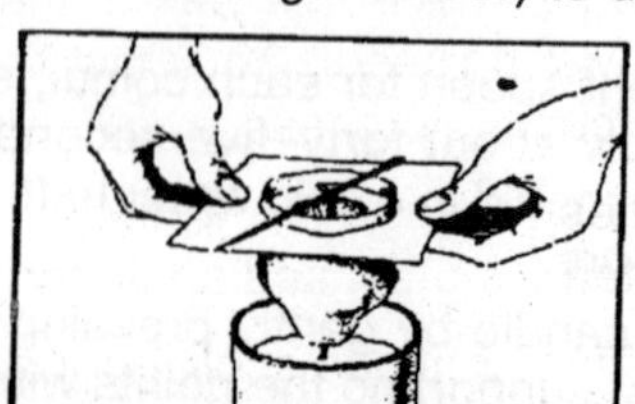

Lowering the mould into the water bath.

METHOD

1. Melt the wax in the double boiler and stir in the 'pear fruit' dye.
2. Use the wicking needle to thread the unprimed wick up through the mould. Rest the needle across the base of the mould and tie the wick to it. Gently pull the wick tight.

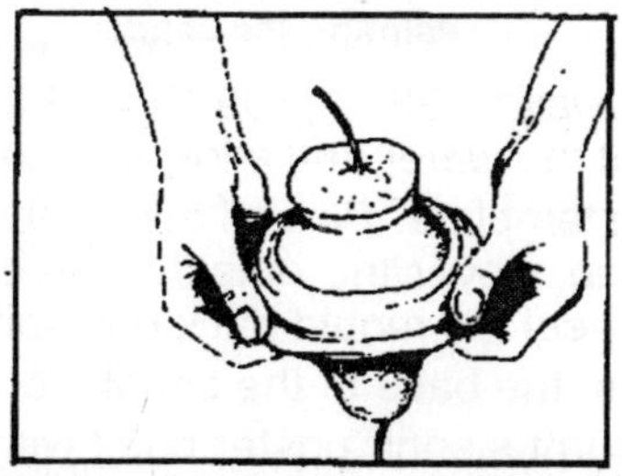

Peeling the mould back on itself.

3. Fit the template around the neck of the mould, and then stand the mould in the empty dipping can.
4. Heat the wax to 93°C (199°F) and pour it into the mould covering the top of the neck. Wait for one minute.
5. Carefully lift the mould up by the tamplate and tap it with a finger to release any air bubbles. Lower the mould into the water bath.

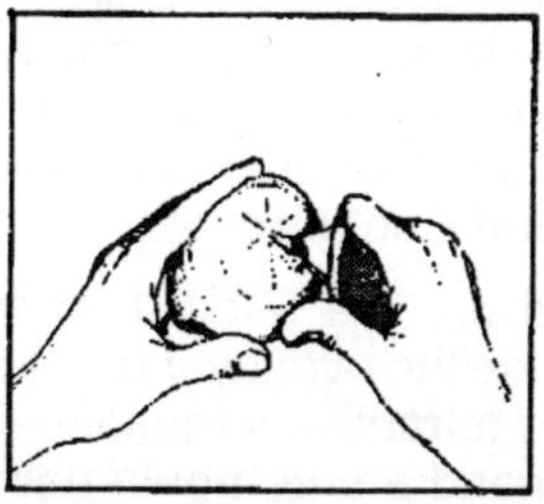

Trimming the base of the candle.

6. As soon as the surface of the wax at the neck starts to solidify, prick it with the wicking needle. You must keep breaking this surface throughout the cooling process.
7. After ten minutes, change the water in the bath. Do this again after a further ten minutes, and again ten minutes later.
8. Allow the mould to continue cooling for another hour and a half. Break the surface at the neck every fifteen minutes or so.

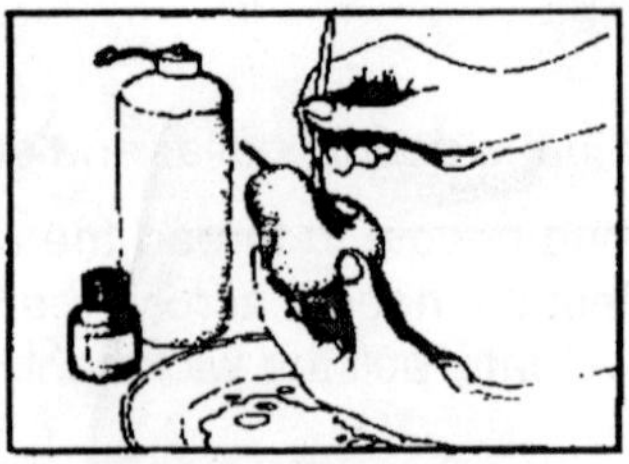

Painting the candle.

9. Reheat the wax to 93°C (199°F) and top up the mould. Lift the mould out of the water and allow it to cool for one hour.
10. Remove the template. Pick off any lumps of wax that have leaked out of the top. Cover the outside of the mould with washing-up liquid, then peel the mould back on itself to remove the candle.
11. Carefully trim the base of the candle to a rounded shape.
12. Mix some burnt sienna poster paint with a little water and add a drop of washing-up liquid. Brush the mixture over the whole surface of the candle and allow it to dry. Wipe off any excess colour with a cloth dampened with white spirit.
13. For the final realistic shine, dip the finished candle in green or yellow wax heated to 82°C (180°F) for four seconds. Wait for one minute, then re-dip for two seconds. After ten minutes, polish your pear with a wet tissue.

Pour–in pour–out candles

This technique is exactly the opposite of overdipping. By pouring in and pouring out, layers of wax are built up on the inside of a mould. It is possible to have as many layers as you like, but author found that good results can be obtained with just two. When preparing wax for this type of candle, remember that the second pour (the underlayer) must be strongly dyed if the colour is to show through. Four times the normal amount of dye will give you colours of sufficient strength.

Any type of mould can be used. Flexible moulds give especially interesting results, because the overlayer tends to be thicker in some places than others. This creates attractive variations in the colour show-through. For beginners, I recommend a star mould because its shape permits the wax to cool quickly and the process can be watched.

The amount of time needed for the first layer to form can be as little as one minute or as long as twenty minutes, depending upon the cooling rate of the mould. As a guide, the overlayer should be about 3mm ($\frac{1}{8}$ in) thick.

How to–pour–in pour–out candle

EQUIPMENT AND MATERIALS

As for an ordinary moulded candle, but with enough wax to fill the mould twice (once with each colour). If you are using a flexible mould, then you will need a stand to hold the mould upright.

METHOD

1. Wick up the mould and fill it with wax at 82°C (180°F). Wait for a 3mm (⅛ in) layer to set.
2. Pour off all the wax that has not solidified and wait for a few minutes.
3. Fill the mould with wax of the second colour at 82°C (180°F) and allow it to cool.
4. After two hours, prick the well and top up with wax at 82°C (180°F). Allow the candle to cool for a further two hours before removing it from the mould.

Making your own moulds

Simple moulds can be improvised from household packaging, such as yoghurt pots and toothpaste pumps, but please take care as hot wax can be very messy. Here is a simple 'rule of thumb' – if it will hold boiling water without collapsing, then you can use it as a candle mould, always remembering, of course, that you have to be able to remove your candle after it has cooled. Shapes that are larger at top than they are at the base cannot be used. Think about it!

Corrugated cardboard makes excellent candles. The only real problem is finding a way to shape and seal the 'top' end and stabilize the wick. For a conical top, the end of a washing-up liquid bottle can be taped to the end. For a flat-topped candle, you will need to cut a circle of thin plastic and make a hole in the centre with a wicking needle.

Spherical moulds can be made from old tennis balls. Cut the ball into two halves. In the centre of one half, make a hole about 3cm (1¼in) in diameter through which to pour the wax. In the centre of the other half, make a tiny hole for the wick. Tape the two halves together and wick up the mould as normal.

Once you have gained confidence, you may wish to try making your own moulds from instant moulding compounds. A number of these are available from good craft shops, and, whilst you should follow the instructions provided exactly, the basic principle is the same. The object to be moulded is coated with release agent, and is then covered with a layer (or several) of moulding compound. The compound is allowed to set (usually for about one hour), and then the mould is gently peeled off. Depending upon the type of compound used, it should then be treated as a PVC or rubber mould.

Mastery of this technique opens up enormous possibilities-candle sculptures, candle china dogs, candles busts of great composers, candle wine bottles, even candles of your own (or a friend's) hand or foot!

8

SURFACE TECHNIQUES

Casting a candle is only half the story. In many respects, a freshly cast candle is just the raw material for the candle-finisher's craft. In this section, we described a number of basic techniques for enhancing and embellishing the appearance of a candle. In the following section, we take this a stage further. With some candles, making the candle and finishing it are part and parcel of the same creative process.

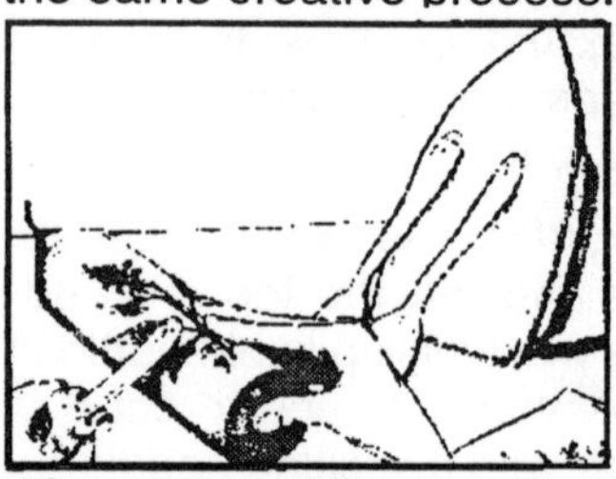

Attaching a pressed flower to the candle.

Pressed flowers and grasses

These should be prepared at least one week before we intend to use them. Wild grasses can be used, but if we are going to use flowers then please buy cultivated flowers from a stall or shop. Do not pick wild flowers.

How to – pressed flower candle

Equipment and Materials

Electric iron; three teaspoons; cloth; thermometer; dipping can containing sufficient undyed paraffin wax to cover the candle; pressed flowers; candle to be decorated.

Method

1. Set the iron on a medium heat and rest the teaspoons against it to heat them up.
2. Take one of the flowers and position it on the surface of the candle.
3. Take one of the spoons and press it all over the flower, melting it

into the wax. Hold the spoon in a cloth to prevent burning our fingers.

4. Repeat with the other flowers in the arrangement, changing spoons as they cool down.
5. Heat the wax in the can to 96°C (205°F) and dip the candle for three seconds. Press down any petals or leaves that are sticking out and dip again for two seconds. At first the wax will be opaque, but it will clear as it cools. Stand the candle on its base and leave it for half an hour before handling.

Applique

With this technique, chunks of coloured wax are stuck on to the outside of a white candle. As the candle burns down, the flame illuminates the chunks from the inside, and they glow as if the candle was studded with uncut gems.

Applique works best with chunks that are strongly coloured but are still translucent. If too much dye has been used, then the chunks will be opaque.

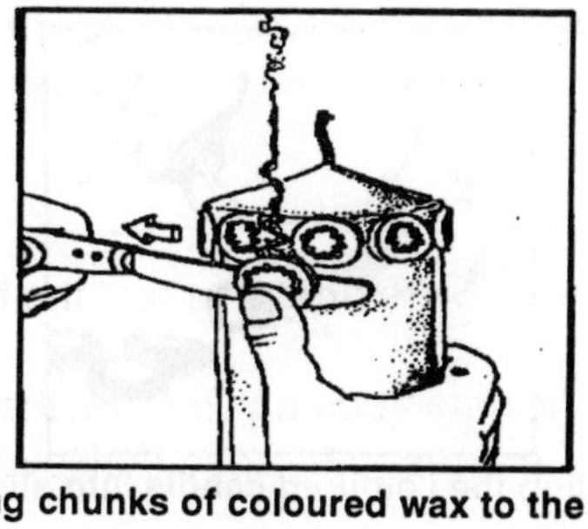

Attaching chunks of coloured wax to the candle.

The process is very simple. All we need is a bowl of water at 96°C (205°F) and a round-ended kitchen knife. Heat the blade in the water, dry it on a kitchen towel, then press the flat of the blade against the candle, holding a chunk of wax against the other side. Slide the blade from between them, and the chunk will stick to the candle. Alternatively, use wax glue. After we have covered the candle, we can dip it in undyed wax as for the pressed flower candle.

With practice, we can create designs or even pictures with applique chunks. As your candle burns down, it will reveal a 'stained glass window' of coloured wax.

Right : a detail of an appliqued candle.
Far right : a selection of appliqued candles

Inlays

This is not strictly a finishing technique, but we have included it here because it is a surface effect. Basically, pieces of contrasting wax are stuck to the inside of a mould before it is filled. When the mould is removed, the wax pieces are revealed as inlays in the surface of the candle. The bull's-eye candle is an attractive design, with a slightly spooky effect when lit that children seem to love.

Cutting the coloured candle into slices.

How to – bull's eye candle

EQUIPMENT AND MATERIALS

Double boiler; thermometer; three dipping cans; mould 12.5cm (5in) square; wicking needle; water bath; weight; sharp knife; electric iron or white spirit; mould seal; one coloured dipped candle 2cm ($\frac{3}{4}$in) in diameter; dyed wax in three different colours for overdipping; 150g (5oz) paraffin wax; 15g ($\frac{1}{2}$oz) stearin; 17cm (6$\frac{3}{4}$in) length of 3.75cm (1$\frac{1}{2}$in) wick; wax glue.

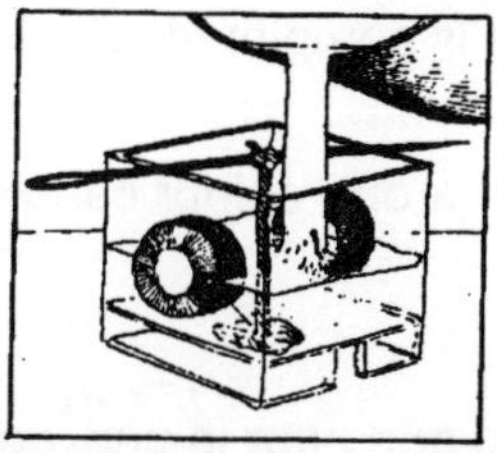

Pouring the wax/stearin mixture into the prepared mould.

METHOD

1. Overdip three additional colours on to the candle. Three three-second dips in each colour should be sufficient. The final diameter should be approximately 3.5cm (1$\frac{1}{2}$in).
2. Allow the candle to cool, then cut two 2.5cm (1in) slices. With a drop of wax glue, stick these in the centre of opposite faces of the mould. Wick up the mould as normal.
3. Heat the paraffin wax and stearin to 82°C (180°F) and pour it into the mould. Tap out the air and place the mould in the water bath.
4. After forty minutes, prick the well and top up with wax at 93°C (199°F). Allow it to cool completely.
5. After removal from the mould, the sides of the candle can be smoothed against a warm electric iron, or polished with white spirit and buffed with a wet tissue.

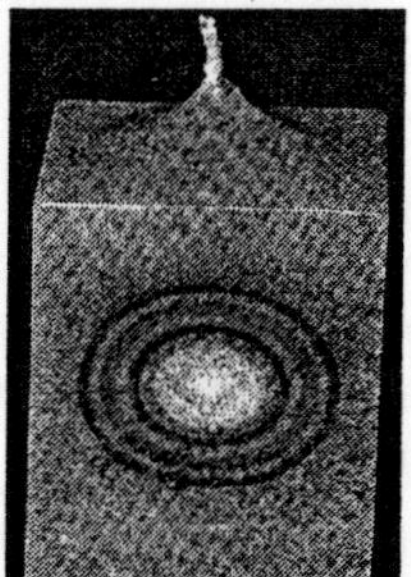

Bull's-eye candle.

Carving

Wax is extremely easy to carve, and we can practise on any old candle or lump of wax. As to what to carve with, use whatever gives the best result – craft knives, penknives, ends of spoons. we can even buy sets of wax carving tools, but we are unlikely to need these unless we are planning a series of family portraits in candles.

The secret is to remove only small pieces of wax at a time. Remember that once we have carved it off, we cannot stick it back, so plan carving carefully. When our design is completed, burnish the carved surfaces with a rounded teaspoon handle.

With this variation on a one-colour candle, we can combine carving with colour.

METHOD

1. Wick up the mould and pour in undyed wax. Allow it to cool until a layer about 5mm (¼in) thick has solidified on the sides.
2. Pour the liquid wax back into the pan, dye it strongly and heat it to 88°C (190°F). Pour the coloured wax into the mould, then cool and top up as normal.
3. When the candle is completely cold, a design can be carved through the plain wax to reveal the colour beneath.

Carved candle

Dip and Iron Back

The electric iron was a great invention for candlemakers. It is a handy tool which provides a smooth heated surface that is superb for removing wax to a uniform level. Candles with a high relief surface can be overdipped in a contrasting colour, which is then ironed away from the high points of the design to reveal the colour beneath.

With very high relief surfaces, more than one colour can be overdipped. It is best to overdip darker colours before lighter ones.

A Selection of candles made by the dip and iron back method

METHOD

1. Each coloured layer needs at least three dips of three seconds each, with one minute between dips.
2. After each colour layer, the candle should be cooled in cold water for five minutes, then dried thoroughly before dipping in the next colour.
3. The iron should be set on a medium heat, and we should work over a tray or sheet of newspaper to catch the drips of wax. Apply the candle to the iron, not the iron to the candle.

Overdipping the candle.

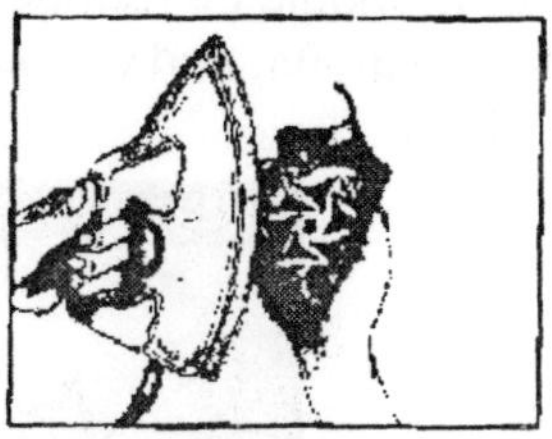

Ironing the candle.

Hammering

Wax is a soft material and care has to be taken against accidental knocks which leave unsightly dents in a candle. This ability of wax to receive an impression when struck can be exploited to excellent decorative effect by hammering.

One of our favourite finishes is that obtained by using a ball-peen hammer. This work especially well on round candles, but care has to be taken to get the spacing equal.

Place the candle comfortably in the lap and lay the ball of the hammer against it. Give the hammer a sharp tap with a mallet or block of wood, not with a metal object. The ball will leave a smooth rounded impression. Repeat the process to build up an overall pattern.

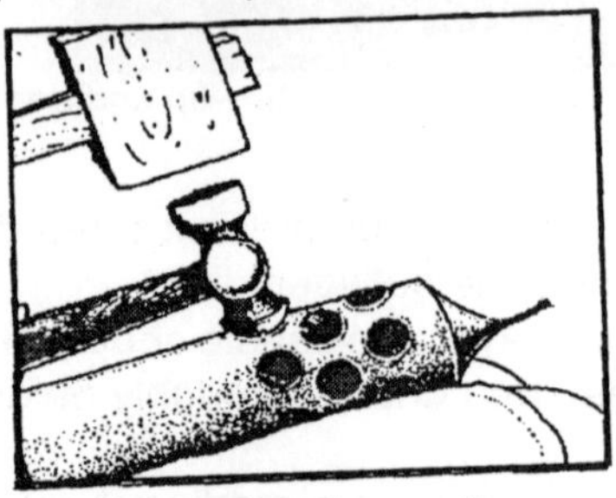

Hammering the candle.

Objects other than a ball-peen hammer can be used to make impressions, but they should be rounded to avoid breaking up the surface. Old bath taps, brass buttons, and various bits of kitchen equipment can all be used to good effect.

Painting

Wax is the best medium for painting on wax. We can use acrylic paint, but we do not recommend it because it can interfere with the smooth burning of the candle.

Any type of wax will do, but beeswax is best, and it can be coloured any shade we choose. It is important to colour the wax with candle pigment because dyes tend to migrate. The wax must be kept warm whilst we paint and an egg poacher is ideal for this. Use an ordinary artist's paintbrush and work with swift smooth strokes, one stroke at a time. The wax cools quickly, so we will need to re-dip the brush frequently. When re-dipping, leave the brush in the wax for at least twenty seconds, so that any wax that has solidified on the brush is completely melted. For speed, use two brushes alternately.

Once we have painted wax on to a candle it can be difficult to remove. We can allow the wax to cool and then rub it off with white spirit, but this will probably mar the surface of the candle. To avoid this, practise our design on a sheet of glass or mirror. Afterwards, the wax can be removed easily with hot water.

Painting the candle.

9

NOVELTY CANDLES

Whatever the end product, a simple dipped candle or a multi-layered landscap, candlemaking is always an enjoyable experience. There is something deeply satisfying about the smell of hot wax and the alchemical combination of ingredients, timing, and temperature.

In this final section, we collected together a number of different techniques which greatly extend the scope of creative candlemaking. For want of a better word, we call them novelty candles because they are an ideal way of celebrating both large and small occasions–a loved one's birthday, a children's party, or one of those wonderful afternoons when we have the time and the inclination to create something really special.

In most cases we detailed instructions for making one particular candle, but do not be afraid to adapt, experiment, or create our own entirely new designs.

Whipped wax candles

As it cools, liquid wax can be beaten or whipped into a froth like the white of an egg. The easiest method is to use an old kitchen fork. Whipped wax behaves rather like whipped cream and can be sculpted into gravity-defying shapes. Whipped wax has the added advantage of setting hard at room temperature. The cooled wax has an attractive surface texture which can be exploited to good effect.

How to-ice-cream cone

Equipment And Materials

Double boiler; fork; dessertspoon; 100g (3½oz) paraffin wax; red dye; triangular piece of beeswax sheet with sides measuring 12.5 cm (5in).

A mouth-watering ice-cream candle, with a chocolate flake made from strips of brown modelling wax.

METHOD

1. Roll the piece of beeswax sheet into a cone and pinch the seam closed.
2. Melt the paraffin wax and remove it from the heat. Once a skin has formed, beat it with a fork until it is stiff, then spoon it on to the top of the cone and shape it as desired. A trickle of wax dyed bright red can provide a touch of mouth-watering strawberry topping.

Birthday cake candles

Parents, partners, and professional pastry-cooks often spend a great deal of time trouble decorating thematic birthday cakes, e.g. an electric guitar, a cricket pitch, the green at the 16th hole, and so on. With a little imagination and creative endeavour, your can create candles to enhance almost any commemorative cake. Whatever the end product, have make the basic candle by dipping. Use a fine grade of wick, such as 1.25 cm (½in), because you are only making very small candles. Various methods can be used for shaping them.

Birthday cake candles.

- Selective dipping produces blobs on the end that can be pressed into the heads of golf clubs.
- Pulling the candle between your thumb and two fingers produces a cricket bat with the authentic V-shaped back.
- Pressing the upper part of the candle flat and trimming it to shape can produce a tennis racket or a guitar.

Once cool, the candle can be painted with coloured wax.

Balloon Candles

This is tricky technique, but worth taking the time and trouble to master. It produces lovely round candle with a translucent surface over swirls of bright colour. As you experiment, you will learn a lot about the physical properties of wax, especially its strengths and weakness.

Balloon candles involve very thin shells of wax, and even experts break a few now and then. The shells can also be deformed by holding them too firmly or for too long in warm hands. Once you have dented a shell, the dent is impossible to remove. Working in the airstream of an electric fan helps to keep the shells cool and firm.

How to-balloon candle

Equipment And Materials

Double boiler; thermometer; four teaspoons and a tablespoon; egg poacher; wicking needle; 1kg (21b 3oz) paraffin wax; four contrasting dyes; 12.5 cm (5in) length of 5 cm (2in) wick; balloon that forms a suitable shape when party filled with water.

Filling the ballon with water.

Method

1. Melt the wax and heat it to 82°C (180°F).
2. Pour small quantities of wax into the egg poacher, dye them, and keep them liquid.
3. Fill the balloon with water until it is about 10 cm (4in) in diameter. Hold the neck tightly closed, and dry the balloon thoroughly with a tissue.

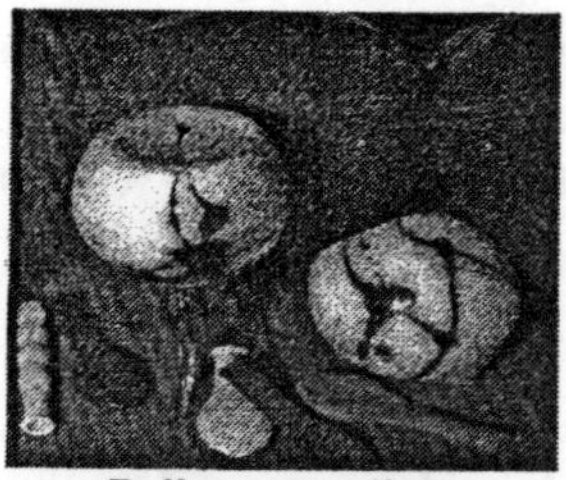

Balloon candles.

4. Dip the balloon into the wax ten times, allowing thirty seconds between dips. Working with only six dips gives a better result, but it is very difficult to do because the wax is so thin.
5. Carefully let the water out of the balloon, and gently remove the balloon from the wax shell.

Dipping the balloon into the wax.

6. Spoon small amounts of dye into the shell and swirl them around the inside. As you work, blow into the shell to cool the dye.

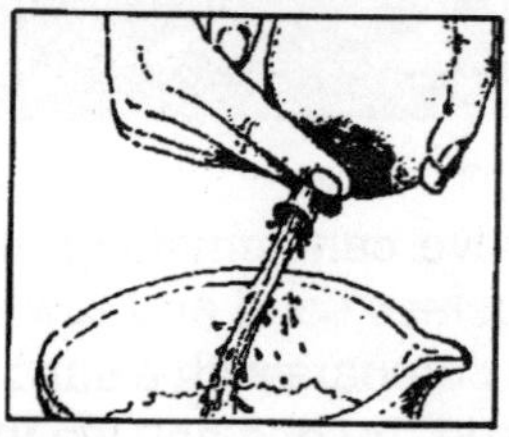

Removing the water from the balloon.

7. When you have laid down sufficient colour, begin to fill the shell with undyed wax using the tablespoon. Add one spoonful of wax at a time and swirl it around the inner surface. Pour any excess back into the double boiler. Slowly build up layers of wax until the shell is about 1.25 cm (½in) thick.

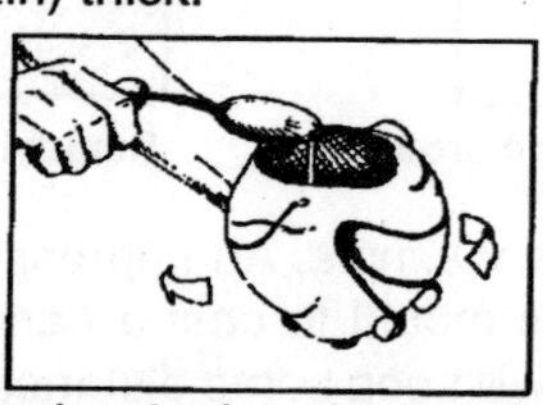

Spooning dye into the wax shell.

8. Prime the wick and, with the wicking needle, carefully thread the wick down through the top of the shell. Attach the wick as with moulded candles, taking care not to damage the wax shell.

Filling the wicked-up candle shell with wax.

9. Fill the candle with wax one tablespoon at a time, allowing each spoonful to set and cool before adding the next.

10. Allow the finished candle to cool for one hour before buffing the surface with a wet tissue.

Sand Candles

These represent creative candlemaking at its very best – creating beautiful candles from shapeless sand and raw wax. For sheer flickering, glowing beauty, nothing can compare with a sand candle as the light soaks through the outer layer of sand. Try one and we think we will agree with us.

Packing The damp sand around the wooden block.

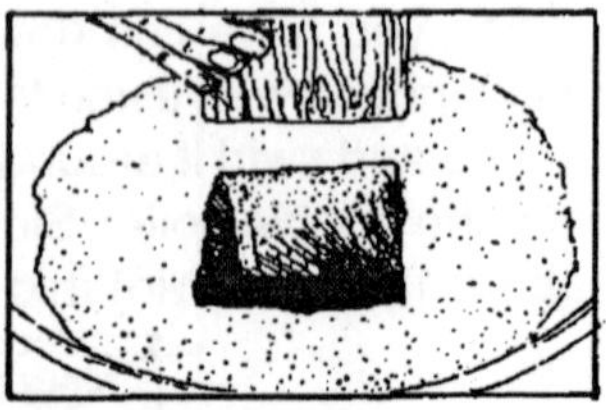

Removing the wood from the sand

Sand candles are very simple. An impression is made in wet sand, and then this is used as a mould to cast a candle. Depending upon the temperature of the wax, it will seep some distance into the sand, creating a crusty coating that can be shaped and carved be hand. Because the sand mould is used only once, you are not limited to shapes that can be lifted cleanly out of the mould. If you can get the shape to stay in damp sand, then you can cast it in wax. Different grades of sand provide different texture and colours. Use as little water as is necessary to get the sand to stay in shape. Generally, 140 cm³ (¼pt) of water to half a bucket of dry sand is about right.

The instructions that follow are a guide to one particular candle, but they can be varied as you wish, for example, as in the star-shaped candles shown above. The important point to remember is that the hotter the wax, the more it will seep into the sand.

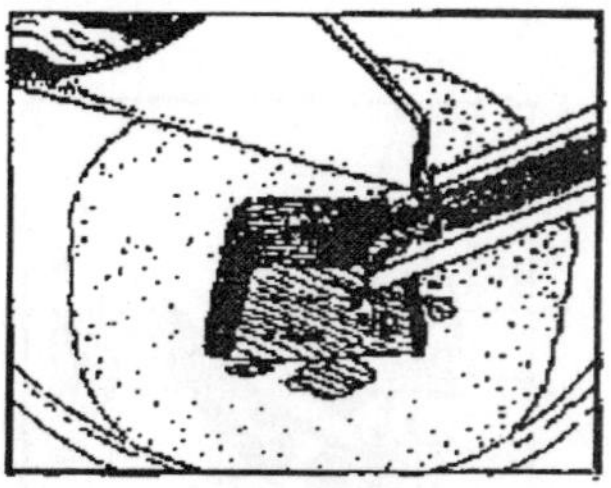

Pouring the wax over the thermometer into the sand mould.

How to–sand candle

Equipment And Materials

Saucepan; thermometer; long wicking needle; pair of dividers for marking out design; surface-forming tool or rasp; carving tools; electric iron; block of wood 20 x 7.5 x 7.5 cm (8 x 3 x 3in); 2kg (41b 6oz) paraffin wax containing 1 per cent beeswax yellow dye; 24 cm (9½in) length of 5 cm (2in) wick; half a bucket of damp sand.

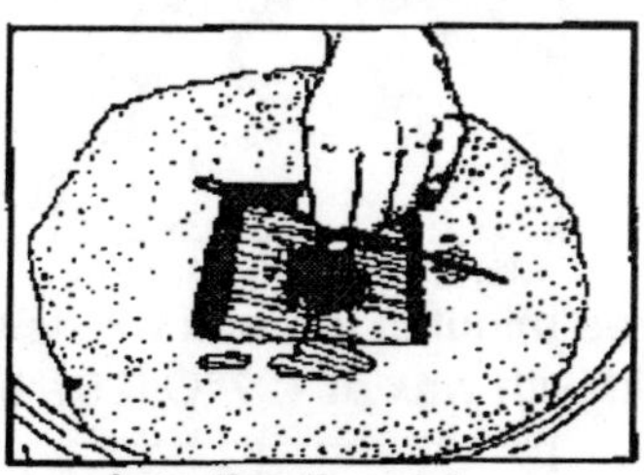

Inserting the wick.

Method

1. Put a 7.5 cm (3in) layer of sand in the bottom of the bucket, and place the block of wood centrally on top of it. Pack the rest of the sand around the wooden block, then tap the bucket sharply on the floor to pack the sand firmly.

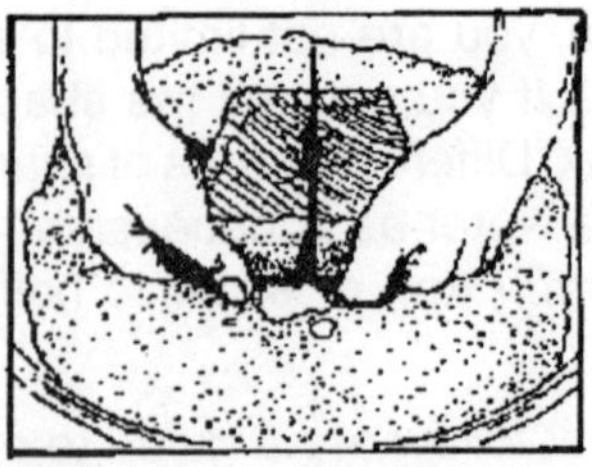

Removing the candle from the sand.

2. Remove the wood from the sand, talking care not to knock any sand from the sides. If you are not happy with the impression, then start again.

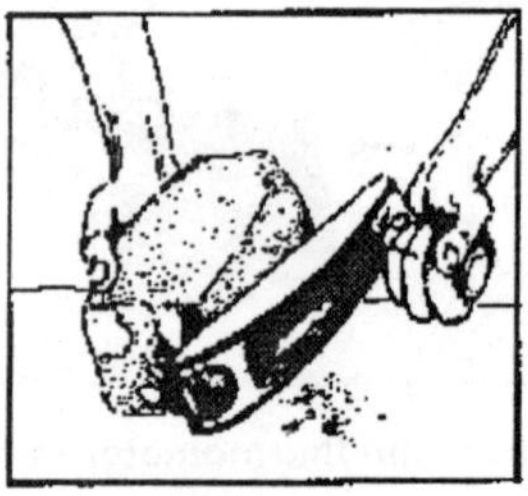

Removing the excess sand.

3. Melt and dye the wax and carefully heat it to 127°C (261°F). Pour the wax over the thermometer into the mould, trying to disturb the sand as little as possible.

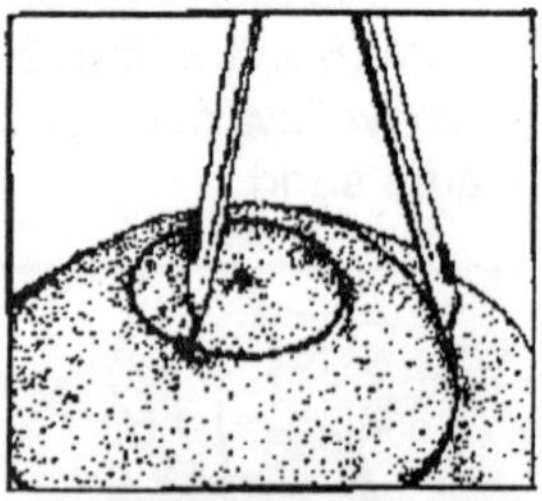

Marking out the design.

4. After about three minutes the wax will have seeped into the sand. Refill the mould with wax at 127°C (261°F) and allow it to cool.

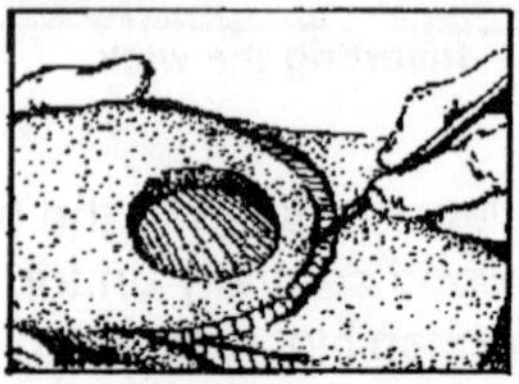

Carving out the design.

5. After two hours, a well will form. Push the wicking needle down through the centre and insert the primed wick. Top up the well with wax at 104°C (219°F) and allow it to cool.

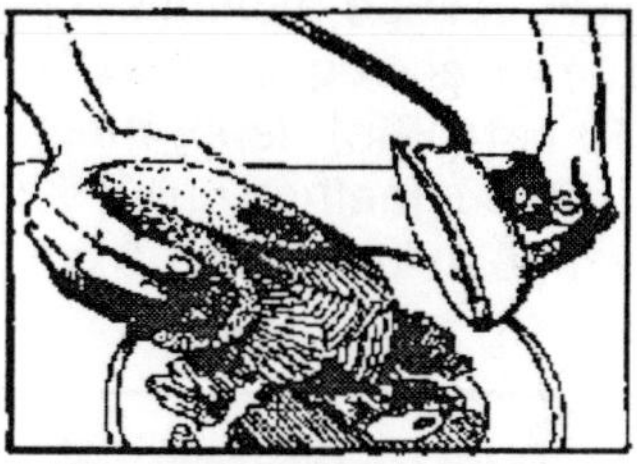

Rounding off the candle.

6. After five hours, remove the candle from the sand. (Because a water bath cannot be used, sand candles take much longer to cool than other candles.)
7. With the surface-forming tool or rasp, remove the excess sand and roughly shape the candle.
8. Mark out the design with the dividers and scratch it into the surface.
9. Carve out the design, then round off the end of the candle with an iron set on a medium heat.

Water Candles

These are quite difficult to make and you will need plenty of practice before you can exert any real influence over the outcome. However, the results can be spectacular – delicate fronds of feathery wax rising from a central core. Because water candles are always somewhat unpredictable, each time that you take the plunge there is the chance of a quite unexpectedly attractive result.

Water candles rely on the fact that wax floats. Hot wax is drawn through cold water, and as the wax rises to the surface it cools and becomes frozen in place. The best results are obtained using specially blended water candle wax and it is not really worth trying this technique with ordinary wax. Always wear rubber gloves when making water candles, as prolonged contact with hot wax at these temperatures will burn your fingers.

Plunge method

Plunging the hot wax into the water.

How to – water candles

Equipment And Materials

There are two closely related methods – plunge and pour – both of which require similar materials and equipments. Double boiler; thermometer; tank of water at least 30 cm (12in) deep; rubber gloves; saucer (plunge method only); pouring jug (pour method only); 500g (1lb 2oz) water candle wax; dipped candle 20 cm (8in) long and 1.8 cm (¾ in) in diameter.

Pour method

Pouring the hot wax on to the candle disc.

Method – Plunge

1. Melt the wax and heat it to 93°C (199°F).
2. Fix a dipped candle to the centre of a saucer, either by melting the end or by using wax glue.

Pushing the candle disc into the water.

3. Fill the saucer with hot wax, then plunge it into the water, twisting it round as you do so.
4. If we are unhappy with the result, then the water candle wax can be melted down and used again. Please take care when remelting the wax, in case any water has become trapped. If the water is allowed to boil, then it will sputter badly.

Method – Pour

1. Melt 80g (3oz) of the wax and pour it into a disc shape, 10 cm (4in) in diameter and 6 mm (¼in) thick. Allow it to cool.

2. Melt the remainder of the wax and heat it to 93°C (199°F).
3. Stick the dipped candle to the centre of the wax disc, and transfer the hot wax to a suitable pouring jug.
4. Holding the edge of the disc at an angle against the surface of the water, pour wax on to the lower edge of the disc.
5. Whilst continuing to pour, push the disc smoothly down and round into the water. A small pool of wax will form on the surface. Continue to pour wax into this pool until that branch of the candle is sufficiently high.
6. Repeat the procedure at other points on the edge of the disc.

Ice Candles

This is a simple technique that is perfect for introducing children to the mysteries of liquids and solids. You start and finish with solid wax and liquid water, but during the candlemaking process you use liquid wax and solid water. Ice candles work because wax forms a skin when it cools. Contact with the ice freezes the wax into shape before the heat of the wax melts the ice. The result is a candle with holes where the ice used to be.

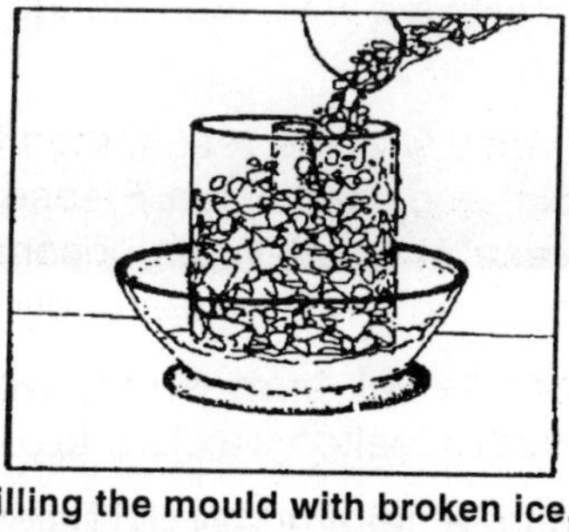

Filling the mould with broken ice.

How to–Ice candle

EQUIPMENT AND MATERIALS

Double boiler; thermometer; cylindrical mould; bowl; 450g (1lb) paraffin wax; brightly coloured dye; 1.25 cm (½ in) diameter candle cut to the same length as the mould; ice broken into 1–2 cm (½-¾in) chunks.

Pouring the wax over the ice.

METHOD

1. Melt and dye the wax, and heat it to 99°C (210°F).
2. Use the 1.25 cm (½in) candle as a wick and insert it into the mould. Make sure that the wick of the candle goes through the hole in the end. Do not use mould seal, as you will want the water to run out.
3. Stand the mould in a bowl and fill it with broken ice, taking care not to disturb the wick candle.
4. With one constant flow, pour the wax over the ice, filling the mould.
5. Leave it to cool for one hour and dry the candle thoroughly before lighting it.

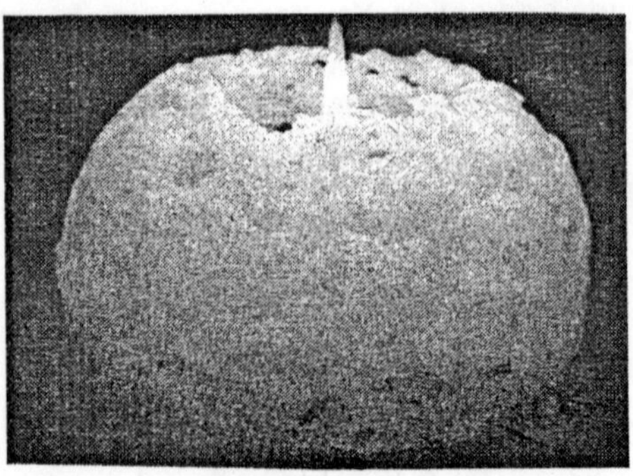

Burning down

A well-balanced candle will burn evenly with a smokeless flame, without producing any excess melted wax to drip or gutter from the candle.

- A candle should be at least a day old before burning.

- Candles should not be burnt in a draught.
- The wick should be trimmed to 1-2 cm (½-¾in) in length.

When a finished candle fails to burn well, there is usually a traceable reason, assuming that you followed carefully all the steps in making it. Listed here are some of the most common burning problems, the probable reasons for them, and what best to do about them.

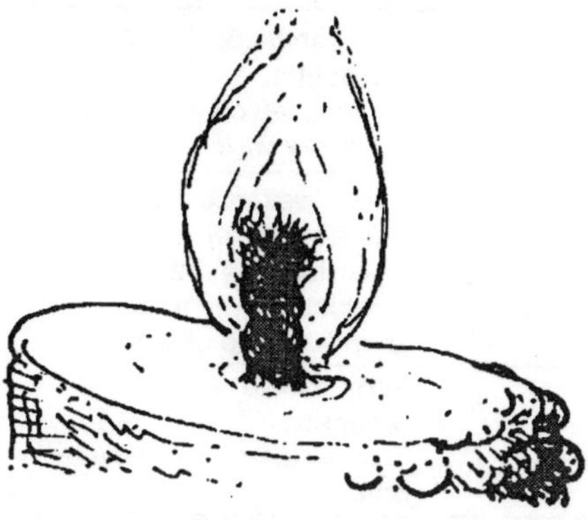

Dipping

Small flame.

Smoking.

Drawning wick.

Burning Flaw	*Cause*	*What to do*
Dripping	Draughts.	Keep candle out of draughts.
	Wax too soft	Check proportions of wax mixture. Use harder wax, or plastics additive.
	Wick poorly positioned or too small	Use a larger wick.
Candle will not burn	Wick unprimed.	Hold candle upside-down and light it.
	Mould seal on wick.	Try to clean off mould seal.
	Water on wick	Try to dry wick.
Small flame	Wax may be too hard	Check wax mixture.
	Wick too small.	Use a larger wick.
	Wick clogged with pigment or dust in candle.	Use wax dyes rather than insoluble pigment, and keep wax free of dust.
Smoking	Draughts.	Keep candle out of draughts.
	Flame not oxidizing well; wick too large.	Trim wick, or use a smaller one.
Wick burns in too small a diameter	Wax too hard. Wick too small.	Check wax mixture, or use a larger wick.
Wick drowns itself in molten wax	Wick too small.	Use larger wick or softer wax.
	Wick seated too loosely in candle.	Improve tension of the wick when wicking up the mould.
	Insolubale pigments used instead of wax dyes.	
Sputtering prevalent ice and water candles	Water in or around wick.	Pour off pool of wax around the wick and relight candle. If it still sputters, then remelt it or throw it away.

10

CHEMICALS COLOURS USED IN CANDLES

Basically colours/dyes are of two types-(1) water solube dyes (2) oil soluble dyes. Water solube dyes are used in colouring textile while oil solube ones are utilizes in colouring oils soaps etc. But the dyes which we use in colouring candles have special properties.

Imperial Chemicals industries Ltd has given special name to such dyes as Waxoline. This dye is available in different shades, by mixing any of these colour shades with the wax manufactures the desired coloured candle very easily. Waxoline is available in the following shades.

Waxoline Yellow

Waxoline Mahogany A.S.

Waxoline Redamine B.S.

Waxoline Orange A.S.

Waxoline Red B.N.A.S.

These dyes are used in colouring oils too. A little quantity is sufficient for the same. About 0.04 gm of the dye is sufficient colour for 800 gms paraffin wax.

Besides, the indegenously made dyes manufactured by shimmal co. of Germany, are also imported for use. The quantity used in colouring is of the order of 1/2 to 100 x parts of the dye to 1000 part paraffin stearine mixture.

In comparsion to paraffin these dyes provide better colour on stearine. These are available in the following shades Red (Sudon-VI) Flexin, Rose,Bengal, Fuchs light.

Yellow (Chinolene Yellow) Auramine Lederine

Green Acid green, Victoria green, Brilliant green.

Blue Induline victoria blue, Methyl violet

These colours/dyes are very very fast.

1-4 ounce of dye is sufficient to colour 112 pounds (1 pound is 16 ounces) stearing. First the stearine or paraffin in which the sye is to be mixed is melted and then the dye which has been emulsified in small quantities of alcohol is mixed in it. If the dye is mixed with alcohol it produces brightness in the wax. Some natural dyes obtained from roots, flowers leaves and dark of plant/trees are also used. Of these natural dyes the under mentioned ones are of special intrest.

1. Ratan Jyot : This is tree whose roots, leaves and bark are dried and ground. This provides red colour when mixed in wax oil. In this process it is preferable to mix the dye in a little quantity of oil/wax and later this colour can be utilized in colouring the rest of the quantity. This is quite an easy and accurate practice to colour oil or wax.

2. Turmeric (Haldi) : To make yellow coloured wax turmeric is powdered and added to molten wax. After 15 minutes it is filtered out through a fine muslin cloth and yellow coloured candles can be easily prepared from this.

3. Chlorophyll Colour : Chlorophyll is a pigment found only in green leaves of any tree. By crushing and grinding thses green leaves, pulp is prepared and later caustic soda to the extent of 0.5% (0.5% of pulp's weight) is added to it. This mixture is stirred to make homogenous and then filtered. After this a sepaerate solution is prepared by mixing sulphuric acid and water (1:4) This solution is mixed with the green solution very slowly (dropwise).

Consequently green colour settles down at the bottom. This green colour is seperated and washed twice or twice or thrice with distilled water. The water is distilled out of it. This green colour is not soluble in but it is easily soluble in wax or oil.

Though these natural dyes do colour the candles but the same invole maintaining precautions and create many problems in their preparation and mixing with the waxes. In comparison to this chemical dyes are cheaper and moreaves only cheap candle require colour whereas good quality candles are generally colourless.

11

CANDLE POWER

The candle of England is taken as the standard unit for the power of light and the same standard has also been taken by Americans. This candles weighs half pound (1 pound = 454 gms). (1 grain = 0.064 gms) and contains 120 grains of spermacete wax as fish oil wax. This candle gets burnt completely in one hour. The quantity of light produced from this candle is taken as a unit. In other words it is called one candle power. In Germany, the candle which is taken as standared is made from paraffin wax and is 20 mm in diameter. It produces a flame which is 20 mm in length.

The unit of light in France is cercel. This unit of France in 9.5 times of English candle and 7.5 times of the light produced by the standard German candles. The measurement of light of the electric bulb is also linked with the candle power viz 40 candle power, 60 candle power and 100 candle power etc. This implies that the light is equivalent to the light produced by 40 candles, 60 candles and 100 candles respectively.

12

WAXES USED IN CANDLES

The candle industry is a major outlet for waxes. Most of the waxes are petroleum based. Now a days mixture of paraffin wax and stearic acid are the most commonly used materials for making candles.The other waxes of minor importance are Ceresin wax, Montan wax, Spermaceti wax and Beeswax, Paraffin wax is comparatively the cheapest wax of all other waxes and the government also provides a quota for the same. All the other conventional waxes have now a days become costly and they are also being used in other industries for manufacturing good quality candles. Often other waxes are also added so as to increase the melting point of the composite mixture. The advantage of increasing the melting point of the wax mixture is that the candles will melt slowly and the candles will not stick to each other in the hot summer season. Besides, the candles will appear more shiny and attractive.

Selection of Good Quality Waxes

For candle making three grades of paraffin wax are ordinarily used

(a) Scale wax

(b) Paraffin wax (50-52°c)

(c) Paraffin wax (53-57°c)

The scale wax is used for glasses. The other two categories of waxes are blended with stearic acid to produce household candles. By adding stearic acid to paraffin wax, the composition is hardened and the bending point is raised. Household candles are made of paraffin wax alone or a mixture of 15% stearic acid and 85% paraffin wax.A composite candle may contain around 30% stearic acid if it is for warm climates, stesine candles may contain as hight as 60-75% stearic acid of paraffin with little or no stesice acid.

For making paraffin candles less prone to bending a small quantity of wax or montan wax may be added. If excess Carnuba wax is used it will result in smoking wet burning and produce a large flame. If montan wax is used the candle produced has an opaque appearance. The other waxes which help in hardening and improving the dripping property of candles are candelilla wax, cetyl alcohol polyethylene wax, palmitic acid stearamide stearone, sterone or plamitone, castor wax etc. With the exception of stearic acid the above materials are only used for specific and speciality uses. The effect of the change in the melting point with the addition of stearic acid is shown as under.

Effect of Blending with Stearic Acid on m.pt

100% Paraffin wax 52°C

90% Paraffin wax + 10% Stearic acid 50.4°C

80% Paraffin wax plus 20% Stearic acid 49.5°C

Ozokerite which has been refined is known as ceresim. It is a suitabe wax for candle making having a high melting point. The candles made from paraffin are more popular due to their good illuminating power and the abscence of the ungent and disagreeable odour that characterises the old stearin candle when it is blown out. Paraffin wax candles have a high degree of lustre combined with translucency and are more adaptable to various decorative shapes and colours etc. With the addition of stearic acid to paraffin wax the tendency of bending in warm weather is reduced. Candles have high melting points and greater illuminising powers compared to paraffin candles and are free from smell. These are greasy to touch and burn with a dry cup and are less prone to dripping unlike ordinary transparent candles.

Church alter candles contain more than 50% beeswax and they may be of white or yellowish Colour.

13

MOULDS AND MACHINES

Candle manufacturing industry is not very much affected by new technologies adopted so far. Still the techniques which were in practice before fifty years, are common practice although some new semi-automatic and fully automatic machines are replacing the old techniques a little bit but not very commonly as they are costlier. In India candle making is started on a cottage scale in the beginning and is at a later stage the increase in production is accomplished by increasing the number of moulds and equipment though the basis remains the same.

In the beginning the wax is to be melted and later it is poured in the moulds which are equipped with threads or wicks. So the basic raw material is wick and wax though wax is of different kinds. The molten wax is poured in the moulds and hence the appartus/equipments for melting and pouring in the moulds are in the main equipment. These are varieties of equipment having different capacities. A description of such vessels/apparatus/equipment is given under:

Heating Elements

Very low temperature is required for melting the wax. The wax melts normaly between 100°F and 150°F temperature, while simple water boils at 212°F. This is the reason why there is no need for any special furnace for the same. One can easily use household *chulha*, stove, cooking gas stove or heater for melting the wax, even a hot water bath can be employed for heating the wax. In this case a tin or bucket(made of M.S) is filled with wax and then put or hung in a water bath (hot) or an immersion rod utilised for heating water may be practiced.

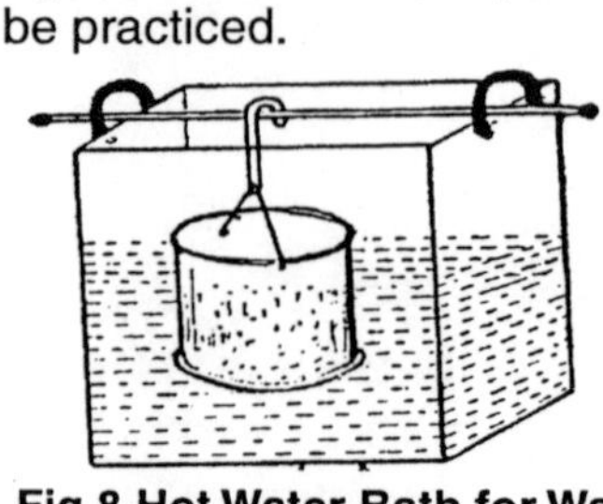

Fig.8 Hot Water Bath for Wax

Melting Vessels

The wax can be melted only when it is in a vessel otherwise it will spread here and there. The size of vessel depends on the quality of wax to be melted.Usually the pan used by confectioners is employed for this purpose.

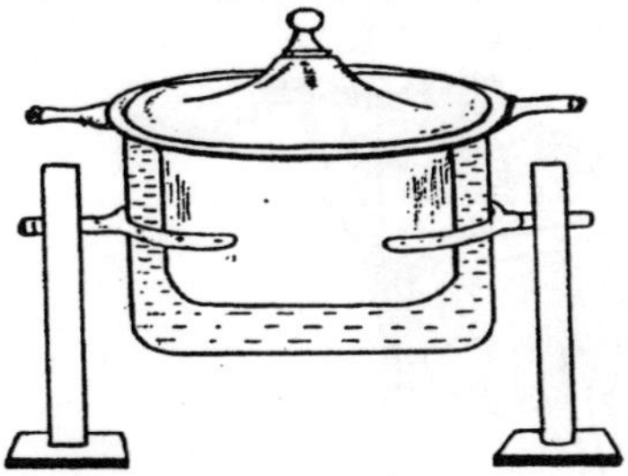

Fig. 9 Jacketted Vessel for Wax Melting

The pan should be such that its base should be heavier or thicker so that the wax would remain melted for a longer time. Also there are few chances of getting the the wax burnt if the vessel is lighter. Wax can burn to make the whole colour very odd and quality also becomes poorer.

Special type of candles viz.idol or toy like are very easily found and for these a number of vessels can be used viz. sauce pan.Aluminium vessels, Teapan or pan etc.Moreover,it is better to heat the water in lieu of wax directly and then a tin or any other vessel containing the wax is put in the pan containing hot water. This way wax can be melted well. In this way there will be no reduction in the quality and quantity of wax melted and the hot water can be used again and again for the same purpose the wax melted this way is fine quality.

Fig. 10 Wax Melting Tank With Heater

For melting purpose a water bath is preferable. It is made of cast iron, and heavy with good shape. Inside the water bath a steel container is fitted. There is a space between the containers. Whenever it is used the empty space is filled with water and the inner container is employed for melting wax.Under the water bath one can put heater or stove. Good quality water bath isequipped with heating elements or immersion rods. Such type of waterbath is called steam jackected pan or water lined steam jacketed kettle.Some models of water bath are equipped with hand operated mixers which enable the operator to mix the wax easily and quickly. The use of water bath saves time, labour as well as space and also it is not very costly.

Fig.11 Water Bath With Mixer

Accessories

The molten wax is poured in the mould with the help of *Dohari* which is made by joining a wooden handle to hemispherical pan. This appears like a big spoon. In lieu of this one can use saucepan or teapan. For stirring purpose big spoons or wooden stick is employed. For peeling purpose one can use knife and pair of scissors can be used for cutting the thread or wick. Besides these one needs buckets, tubs and a thermometer for measuring temperature.

Fig.12 Label For Pouring Molten Wax

Moulds

Moulds are the most important parts of candle indusry. These moulds are made of aluminium and gun metal and posses standard measurements. Gun metal moulds are comparatively heavier and costlier and rarely used. Aluminium moulds are cheaper and lighter. These can be easily closed and opened. Moulds are available in market in different sizes and even you can get them manufacured on order as per your chioce.

The cost of moulds depends upon the productive capacity. Number of candles manufactured in a single turn and the sizes of candles generally 12, 24, 36, 48, 60, or more/fewer candles manufacturing moulds are available in the local market. Moulds with more capacity are comparatively costlier but they give good yeild (output), save labour as wll as time.

To make use of locally avaiable moulds as acommon practice for manufacturing fancy candles. Some ambitious, and creative persion go for new design and shapes. They use moulds of earth, plaster of paris or plastic. Defacto moulds are the basis of candle industry.

Automatic & Semi Automatic Machines

If you want to increase the yield you have to use semiautomatic or automatic machines which can enhance the state of production. One machines can manufacture only one size of candle when machines are used. Machines are employed only when a large production is desired. Only one man can handle the whole work. The wax used is feeded in the feeder and valve of steam pipe is opened. Consequently hot steam enters the machine and melts the wax. This melted wax get filled up itself in the moulds and later the valve through which cool water is to come is opened which cools down the moulds resulting in the solidification of candles to check whether the wax is solidified or not there is a thermometer fitted in the machine. When it showes 30° C it is meant that the wax in the mould has been solidified and candles are manufactured.

After this,handle of the machine is moved which makes the piston filled with the moulds to push out the candles. These candles are jointless clean smooth and regular. But you can also manufacture fancy or special candles using these machines.

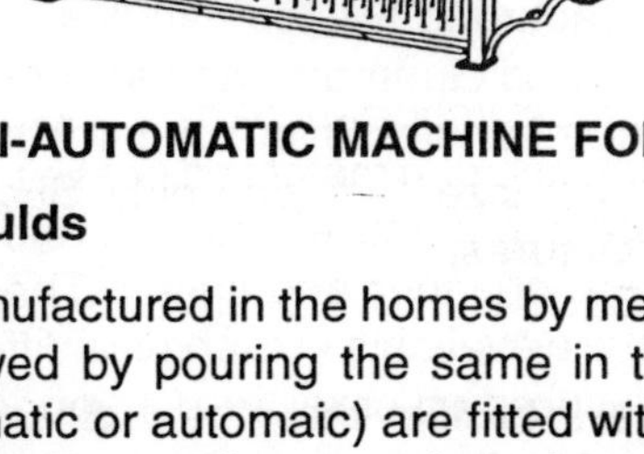

Fig.13 SEMI-AUTOMATIC MACHINE FOR CANDLE MAKING

Classification of Moulds

Candles are manufactured in the homes by melting ordinary vessels or in waterbath followed by pouring the same in the moulds. Even the machines (semiautomatic or automaic) are fitted with the special types of moulds, the moulds used in candles manufacturing are of Brass. Ordinary moulds have then described earlier. Here we are giving an account of some modern moulds in this section.

Moulds With Water Tank

In ordinary moulds the wax is filled up in the same order and allowed to cool down to get solidified candles.

These moulds are equipped the water container which we call water tank. There is no need of seperate tube in these moulds.One more facility is there in these moulds that they are not displaced as already a tank is attached.

During operation the water of tank gets warmed then this water is emptied out and cool water is filled in lieu of that moulds having water tank create a little difficulty because the quantity of cooling water is very less and consequently gets warmed and has to be changed. This way there is a loss of time.These moulds are heavier as well as costlier. Even operation is tedious therefore the practice of using moulds is reducing day by day.

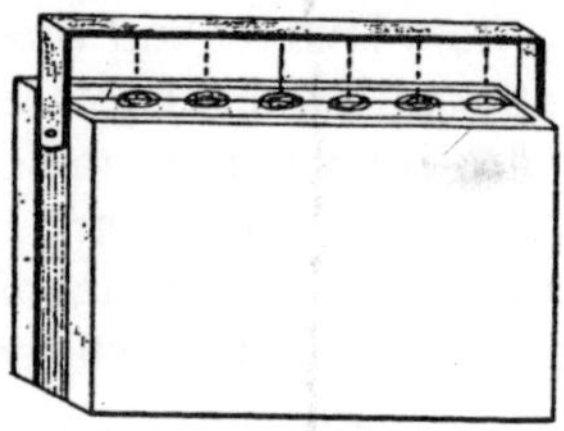

Fig.14 Simple Mould For Making

Special Size Moulds

Now a days the candles of large sizes are more popular. Aluminium or Gunmetal moulds are easily available to manufacture 30-35 cm long and 2.5 cm thick candles.50 cm long into 4 cm thick or a very large sized candles making moulds can also be purchased from the market or one can order for the same as this can easily be fabricated.

Moulds for Twisted Candles

Moulds for manufacturing twisted candles are unlike ordinary ones and made of aluminium and Gunmetal, and are costlier. In our country this type is mould for little size candles. In our country these type of candles are generally made in 18 cm size.7cm long only. Such types of moulds are popular among manufactures.

Special moulds

Fancy Candles are costlier than the ordinary ones. These candles are thick and long that is why more wax is employed which increase the production cost. These all factors collectively increase the market value of these candles. Candles with designs are made by using clay moulds also as well as moulds of aluminium gunmetal. Gunmetal moulds are costlier in comparison to clay mould. One designed mould can manufacture, one candle at a time.Clay moulds are cheaper as well as the design is simple which enables the manufacture to handle the same with ease. Like metal moulds, clay moulds also consists of two parts.Half of the design is one part and other half is second. When the parts are seperated the moulds gets opened. The top and bottom parts of the moulds are equipped with a small hook made up of in wire in which a wick is inserted.

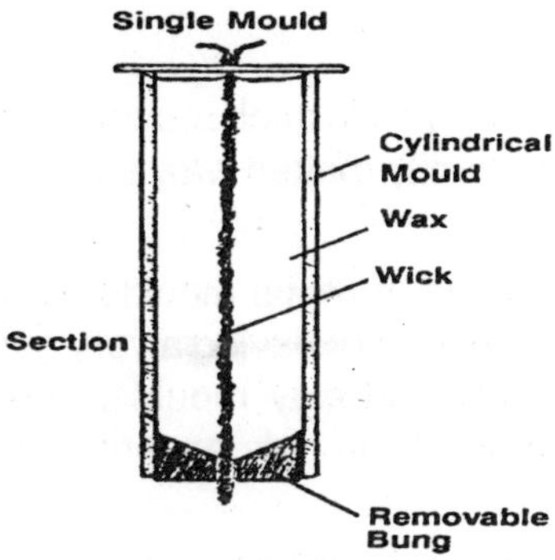

Fig.15 Moulds for Making Four or Six Candles at a Time and not Very Much Costlier

Hand Made Moulds *(Plaster of Paris Moulds)*

Moulds made up of metals are being prepared by dye makers (Fabricators)and clay moulds by potters. We can also make moulds ourselves using plaster of paris. This practice is rather good as well as cheaper. This can make one able to manufacture variety of candles with different designs.

Procedure

To prepare such mould the basic raw material is plaster of paris. Firstly, choose the model to be made viz. an idol, toy, flower or anything else. Now take a shallow tray. Add plaster of paris in it and pour water so that it becomes like wet flour slurry for making chapatties. Now place the toy and press it in the wet plaster of paris till it inserts in the same just half, within a minute the plaster will be dry. Take out the toy as well as the half mould from the tray and repeat the same for making another half mould in the same way. For better and easier way to get the moulds out from the tray, it is suggested to cover the wet plaster of paris by a fine cloth, paper or a polythene sheet.Moreover one can apply grease or vaseline in the tray. When these moulds are dried up fully they are made smoother with the help of sand paper and a channel is made in the moulds with the help of a rasp for wax filling. Also at the joint a thin channel is made for setting the wick in the same.

Use of Various Things/Articles as Moulds

Using imagination as a number of things viz,. port, fancy glass items, ashtrays etc.can be used as moulds to form base for fancy candles. Similarly plastic toys (Hollow) which depict clear shapes and curves can be cut in two equal parts vertically or horizontally as desired. Even empty egg shells can be used in manufacture.

Spherical Candles

In order to insert thread or wick in such moulded articles a hot needle can be employed and subsequently molten wax is poured to keep the wick secure.

Ordinary candles are made in metal moulds mostly. Fancy candles gain good profitability but these are not having a very good sale. During the use of plaster of paris moulds and clay moulds, care should be taken because they can easily break. Thus only experienced hands should go for the same.

The use of these moulds is good,because one can easily introduce new mould of candles without investing enough money labour as well as time. This way one can earn more profits,can beat the competition.

14

SELECTED FORMULATIONS

1.	Paraffin wax	Wax melting at (M.pt 135°-140°F)	80 Parts
	Stearic acid	(Triple Pressed)	20 parts
2.	Paraffin wax	(135°-140°F)	90 Parts
	Stearine	(Triple Pressed)	10 Parts
3.	Paraffin wax	(135°-140°F)	70 Parts
	Stearic acid	(Double Pressed)	30 Parts
4.	Paraffin wax	(M.pt.135°-140°F)	85 Parts
	Bees Wax		5 Parts
	Stearic acid	(Double Pressed)	10 Parts

Note : Formulation No 3 & 4 produces candles which melt at lower temperature in comparision to the other prepared using (1) & (2) formulations.

5.	Paraffin wax	(135°- 140°F)	only
6.	Paraffin wax	(125°-130°F)	80 Parts
	Paraffin wax	(135°-140°F)	20 Parts

Formulations No. 5 & 6 are utilised in the manufacture of cheaper quality candles.

Still cheaper candles can be manufactured by using paraffin wax (115°-125°F), these candles are freely available in local markets.

Foreign Type Candles
(Secret formulations)

1. Transparent Candles

Spermaceti and fish wax	90 Pound
Animal fat (purified)	5 Pound
Paraffin wax	5 Pound
FITKARI (Alum)	2 Ounce
Bitartrate of potash	2 Ounce

Procedure

Each type of wax is taken in separate vessels..,After getting it melted in water bath mix it thoroughy.

Later, take 2 ounce Alum and 20 ounce Bitartrate of potash, grind well then mix it in the wax.While mixing stir it constantly and let the heat be high until it is 175°F. Now let the temperature come down till it reaches 149°F so that the dirt could settle in bottom. Seperate out the clean wax pour it in dies (moulds). This way one can get trasparent candles.

2. Milky Candles

The milky candles are prepared by mixing the molten Paraffin, Stearine, Beta-Naphthol Benzoate.

Milky colour can also be achieved by adding Zinc Oxide, Titaniuum Oxide, or Beta-Naphthol to the molten paraffin.

Mix 84 gms Zinc Oxide in a little quantity of molten wax filter through fine cloth then add 1000 gms.paraffin to it.

They will also result in milky appearance of wax.

If 1% Betanaphthol is mixed in melted wax it turns to cloudy white colour. Candles made in this way appear as if stearine is used in them. Alittle quantity of Methylated spirit is mixed in paraffin wax then there appears a brownish colour in the milky wax.

	Part
Paraffin wax	60-70
Stearic Acid	35-40
Paraffin wax	3
Stearic Acid	31
Beeswax	6

Formulation for Good Quality Costly Candles

		Parts
1. Stearic Acid	(Tripple pressed)	70
Paraffin wax		30

	Parts
2. Paraffin wax	80
Stearine	45
Carnoba wax	5

Procedure is same as given earlier for all the above mentioned candles manufacture.

	Parts
3. Paraffin wax	85
Stearic Acid	45

As Paraffin wax is costlier,one can also use the under-mentioned formulation to manufacture candles.

	Gms
4 White Ral Resin	1136
Animal fat	2272
Rice starch	568
Camphor remains	142

Procedure

Melt the fat & mix resin in it later add rice starch and Camphor remains (finely ground) in it.After this prepare the candles with the help of moulds.

	Gms
5 Animal Fat	1600
Boiled potatoes	800
White resin	3200
Turmeric	100
Paraffin wax	200

Procedure

Melt the fat and mix it with white resin.Simultaneously melt the paraffin wax and add it to the same. When all the things are mixed well add finely.

Ground potatoes & turmeric to it & manufacture the desired candles.

	Gms
6. Paraffin wax	800
White resin	200

Melt both of these things and accordingly prepare the desired candle using moulds/dices

Other Formulations for Candle Manufactures

1. Hard Paraffin wax	1500 gm
Stearic Acid	850 gm
Bees Wax	100gm

Procedure

Take a big vessel (Karai) and pour stearic acid and wax in the same. Melt it and then pour the same in dices/moulds having wicks. Place the moulds in a water bath (Tub) to cool the same in order to get the candles hardened. Later bring out the candles moulds & pack the same in packets.

2.	Hard Paraffin wax	40kgs
	Stearine	40kgs
3	Paraffin wax	52kgs
	Stearic acid	40kgs
	Bees wax	4kgs
4.	Bees Wax	64kgs
	Stearic acid	16kgs
	Hard Paraffin	8kgs
5.	Hard Paraffin	71.2kgs
	Stearic acid	15.2kgs
	Pure Carnobawax	800gms
6.	Paraffin wax	47.2kgs
	Vegetable oil	48.8kgs

Procedure

Same for all as given for (1) Case

Milky White Candles

(1)	Hard Paraffin wax	92kg
	Stearine	3.2kg
	Zinc Oxide	800gm

Procedure

Cut the wax in small pieces and get it melted in big vessel (Karai) take about 2.5 kg of this molten wax add the required quantity of zinc oxides till it gets completely dissolved.

Filter the mixture through a fine cloth.Later mix the filtrate in the remaining wax (melted) stir it. Now you can use this candles by filling the same in moulds folliwed by cooling in water bath.

(2)	Paraffin wax	900gm
	Stearic acid	40gm
	Tlurotan	10gm

Procedure

Mix Hurtolan in the melted wax and add stearic acid to the save filter it and use in manufacturing candles.

Hardened Candles *(Having animal fat)*

(1)	Sheep fat	48kg
	Camphor	800gm
	Alum	800gm

Procedure

Fill in the sheep fat and get it melted mix alum in it at last add camphor in the mixture. Now filter the mixture and make candles using the filterate.

(2)	Lard (Pigisfat)	20kg
	Alum	100gm
	Caustic soda	100gm
	Water	200gm

Procedure

Pour the cleaned fat in the vessel and put it on the furance to get it melted. Take a pot with soda and mix alum and caustic soda in the same. Heat the mixture to get a better concentrate till vapours do not appear. Now add this concentrate in the melted fat and prepare the candle accordingly.

Formulations for Making Opaque Candle~

(1)	Paraffin wax	900gm
	Stearic acid	50gm
	White oil	50gm

Procedure

Melt the mixture of above thing at lower temperature then pour it in the mould to manufacture candles.

(2)	Paraffin wax	56kgs
	Stearine	12kg
	White oil	12kg

Procdure

Pour the wax (paraffin) and stearine in an aluminium vessel and get it melted at alower temperature later mix white oil in the same. Stir it well and then prepare candles as desired.

Purification of Wax

Paraffin wax usually gets dirty when it is placed in open. If some dirt settles on this, it can easily be peeled off whenever clean wax is required.

Sometime you can easily get old and wax at cheaper prices. This wax ca be purified by various techniques mentioned as under :

(1) Using Sulphuric Acid : Melt the wax and mix some hot water and sulphuric acid in the same. Stir and cool down the whole. Dirt is collected at the bottom which can easily be seperated off.

(2) Take a little quantity of water and pour dirty paraffin wax in it. Get it melted on then add some potassium Bichromate and sulphuric acid (1% of wax wt). Let it boil for a short while. Here also the dirt will sit in the bottom. For more clear wax, boil it once more with clear water and filter it through a fine cloth.

(3) Fullers Earth is easily available in the market (It is known as Multanimitti or Reh) Usually washer men use it for cleaning purpose as it cuts the dirt. This can also be employed for cleaning and purifying animal fat/oil and wax too and the process is as under :

Take the required quantity of fullers earth and heat the same strongly in a brass or iron sieve. Later pour the melted wax upon this hot earth (fuller earth). The wax will go across the sieve and gets collected in the vessel put under the same. Fullers earth will absorb all the dirt present so far in the wax. To get more clear wax repeat the process. The used fuller's earth can be utilised for many times as the earth can be reactivated every time when it is heated.

15

COLOURED CANDLES MANUFACTURE

In order to prepare coloured Candles viz.blue, red, yellow etc the corresponding Waxoline is mixed. The desired Waxoline is taken in cloth pouch and then immersed in the wax to allow it to mix from all sides. In this way the whole wax gets coloured.

(1) **Blue coloured Candles :** Here Waxoline Victoria Blue is used. One Kg of this is enough for 1000 kgs of wax.

(2) **Green Coloured Candles :** Waxoline green is used in the appropriate quantity of wax.

(3) **Yellow Coloured Candles :** Waxoline Yellow is mixed in the ratio of one kg to 1000 kgs. of wax. The contents are filtered through through a fine cloth & poured into the dices/moulds.

(4) **Red Coloured Candles :** Waxoline Red B.N.S.is mixed in the required quantity of wax to prepare red coloured candles.

(5) **Rose Coloured Candles :** Waxoline Rodamine B.S. is used. Quantity is same as mentioned earlier.

(6) **Orange Coloured Candles :** *I part* Waxoline orange A.S. is mixed with 1000 parts of melted wax to prepare orange coloured candles.

(7) **Mahogany Coloured Candles :** Waxoline Mahogony A.S is used in the same way.

(8) **Violet Coloured Candles :** Waxoline Violet B.S is used in the same way as mentioned earlier.

Tricoloured (National Flag) Candles : Generally candles are manufactured in only one colour, but sometimes for variety sake candles having more than one colour are manufactured. Such candle manufacturing requires wax to be taken in separate vessels with different colour. While preparing tricoloured candles take three separate vessels having melted wax. Mix waxoline green to first, Zinc Oxide or Beta naphthol or Titanium Oxide to the second and add Waxoline orange A.S. to third. Pour the corresonding coloured wax from three vessels in the moulds/dices one after another so that each colour should get 1/3 part of each mould. After pouring wax let the mould cool to get tricoloured candles.

16

PERFUMED CANDLES

If the candles are scented/perfumed, they provide light as well as a good smell. Such types of candles are used in the rooms of patients. The scented candles provides a good aroma and a pleasing atmosphere. Scented/performed candles are common also in temples, mosques and churches.

Perfumed candles making is not a difficult job. The manufacturing process is same and only some perfumes as used in aggarbatties are mixed in the wax with base. These candles are not easily found in the market and thus could prove a profitable industry with good potential. The desired perfume (7 to 14 gms) is mixed in 454 gms of molten wax & then the mixture is poured in the moulds.

17

MEDICATED CANDLES MOSQUITO REPELLENT CANDLES

If a little quantity of citronella oil or orange peel oil is mixed with the melted wax one can easily manufacture mosquito repellent candles. During burning they provides a pleasing smell of orange.

Formulation of Mosquito Repellent Candle

Name	Parts
Candle wax	14400
Waxoline colour (as per choice)	3
Eucalyptus oil	800
Citronella	1200
Stearic acid	400
Camphor (scent)	60

Procedure

Cut the candle wax and stearic acid in small pieces and get it melted. Later mix waxoline colour as per your choice. After this add Eucalyptus oil, Citronella oil as well as Camphor in the melted wax and stearic acid. Stir the mixture till it becomes homogeneous. This melt can now be filled in the dices/moulds to prepare the desired candles. Such candles are inscecticidal also. Mosquittoes dislike the smell and run away. These candles should be packed properly in a waxy paper to retain the presence of perfumes.

18

MAGIC CANDLES (COLOURED FLAME CANDLES)

The candles which impart coloured flames are manufactured by employing different mixtures. A few of these lack wicks and the wax itself gets burnt to yeild coloured flame (light). Such candles are not ideal ones and these can be prepared even dropping the wicks in the concerned chemicals. These candles are not easily available in the market and hence posses a good market potential if introduced properly.

Formulations for Coloured Flame Candles

1. Red Coloured Flame (Light) : Wet the wick in saturated solution of Strontium Nitrate and later use it in candle manufacturing. As this chemical is highly soluble in water it is suggested to prepare the solution having 10-15% chemical in it. Such type of candle imparts red coloured light.

2. Blue Coloured Flame (Light) : 15% Copper Nitrate solution is employed in the preparation of blue coloured flame candles. Procedure is same as above.

3. Green Coloured Flame (Light) : Here we use 15-20%, Barium Nitrate solution.

4. Golden Coloured Flame : Wet the wick in 5-10% Sodium Chloride solution. Dry the wick and prepare the desired candles.

5. Violet Coloured Flame : Prepare 15-20% saturated solution of Potassium Chloride in water and wet the wick in the same. Dry the wick and manufacture the candles. On burning these candles give sharp violet light.

Procedure to Prepare Saturated Solution

Dissolve the required chemical in water, steam or distilled water till it stops getting dissolved. Wicks of cotton are made wet in this solution. This is followed by drying of wicks. Later these wicks are used in manufacturing candles.

19

PROJECT PROFILES

1. Wax Candle (Automatic Plant)

Capacity 500 Kgs/Day

1.	Covered Area	200 Sq. Mts.
2.	No. of Employs..	9 Nos.
		In Lakhs
3.	Land and Building	2.1
4.	Plant and Machinery	0.9
5.	Other Fixed Expenses	0.2
6.	Fixed Capital	3.2
7.	Working Cap/Month	2.9
8.	Working Cap/3 Months	8.7
9.	Margin Money for W/Cap	2.2
10.	Cost of Project	5.4
11.	Total Captial Investment	11.9
12.	Cost of Production	37.0
13.	Sales Receipts/Year	46.0
14.	Gross Profit	9.0
15.	Rate of Return	75.6%
16.	Break Even Point	28.0%

Source of Finance

– Fixed Captial from Financial Institution	2.56
– Working Cap. from Bank	6.53
– Self Raised Finance	2.81
Total	11.90

2. Wax Candle (Manual Plant)

Capacity 220 Kgs/Day.

1.	Covered Area	100 Sq.Mt.
2.	No. of Employees	5 Nos.

		In Lakhs
3.	Land and Building	1.40
4.	Plant and Machinery	0.60
5.	Other Fixed Assets & Expenses	0.20
6.	Fixed Capital	2.20
7.	Working Cap/Month	2.0
8.	Working Cap/3 Months	6.0
9.	Margin Money for W/Cap	1.5
10.	Cost of Project	3.7
11.	Total Captial Investment	8.2
12.	Cost of Production	26.0
13.	Sales Receipts/Year	32.0
14.	Gross Profit	8.0
15.	Rate of Return	97.0%
16.	Break Even Point	30.39%

Source of Finance

18.	Fixed Captial from Financial Institution	1.76
19.	Working Cap. from Bank	4.50
20.	Self Raised Finance	1.94
	Total	8.20

Evidently new entrepreneurs are faced with a situation where they cannot decide how to proceed further in this particular project. The entrepreneurs should go through Practical Project Execution Know How Report, which is prepared by of technocrats and market research analysis supported by a panel of exports equipped with an industrial computerised data bank.

Practical Project Execution Know How Report provides proper way to meet the practical problems which pose difficulities, delays and hike in pre evaluated project cost.

3. Medicated Mosquito Repellant Candles

Capcity 150 kgs/Day 15 mm Dia 195 Length 5000 Nos/Day

1.	Covered Area	300 Sq Mts
2.	No of Employees	4 Nos
		In Lakhs
3.	Land and Building	1.90

4.	Plant and Machinery	0.30
5.	Other Fixed Expenses	0.10
6.	Fixed Capital	2.3
7.	Working Capital/Month	3.2
8.	Working Capital/3 Months	9.6
9.	Margin Money for W/Cap	2.4
10.	Cost of Project	4.7
11.	Total Capital Investment	11.9
12.	Cost of Production	40.57
13.	Sales Reciepts	50.71
14.	Gross Profit	10.14
15.	Rate of Return	85.25%
16.	B.E.P	26.25%

Source of Finance

17.	Fixed Capital from Financial Institution	1.84
18.	Working Cap.from Banks	7.20
19.	Self Raised Finance	2.86
	Total	11.90

Although the brief plant economics given above provides you the cost estimation part of the project, but the before going in for implementation the entrepreneurs are advised to go through Market Survey cum Detailed Techno Economic Feasibility Report, which gives a bird's eye-view of the market survey, all vital project data on the economic capacity,manufacturing process, financial implications, sources of supply of plant and machinery and raw materials etc.

4. Magic Candles (Coloured)

Capacity 600 Kgs/Day 25mm dia x195 mm x 5000 Nos x 90 gms

1.	Covered Area	200 Sq Mts
2.	No. of Employees	14
		Rs. In Lakhs
3.	Land & Building	2.60
4.	Plant and machinery	0.62
5.	Other Fixed Assets & Expenses	0.55
6.	Fixed Capital	3.77
7.	Working Capital/Month	4.36

8.	Working Capital/3 Months	13.08
9.	Margin Money for W/Cap	3.27
10.	Cost of Project	7.04
11.	Total Capital Investment	16.85
12.	Cost of Project	55.50
13.	Sales Reciept	72.0
14.	Gross Profit	16.5
15.	Rate of Return	98%
16.	B.E.P	22.33%

Source of Finance

17.	Fixed Capital from Financial Institution	3.02
18.	Working Cap. from Banks	9.81
19.	Self Raised Capital	4.02
	Total	16.85

The entrepreneurs are often perplexed with certain critical problems. It is part of entrepreneurs ability of constrain those problems and eradicate the faults. In such case the entrepreneurs and industrialists without making any delay should take advantage of Practical Project Execution Know How Report, which will simplify the procedure for assessing market potential, investment decisions making getting various Govt. approvals, registration etc. and loan clearance from financial institutes/Banks.

However, the Practical Project Execution Know How Report can help entrepreneurs expedite the decision making at corporate level and in actual setting up the project.

5.Automatic Cylindrical Candle Making Unit
(Coloured and Plain Candle)

Capacity 4200 Kgs/Day (Candle size 2 cm x 20 cm)
wt.60 Gm/ Candle appx

1.	Covered Area	500 Sq Mts
2.	No. of Employees	16
		Rs.In Lakhs
3.	Land & Building	13.50
4.	Plant & Machinery	155.00
5.	Other Fixed Capital	9.00
6.	Total Fixed Capital	177.50

7.	Working Capital/Month	32.50
8.	Working Capital/3Month	97.50
9.	Margin Money	24.40
10.	Cost of Project	201.90
11.	Total Capital Investment	275.00
12.	Cost of Production/Annum	475.05
13.	Turn Over/Annum	567.00
14.	Gross Profit/Annum	91.95
15.	Profit sale Ratio	16.22%
16.	Rate of Return	33.44%
17.	B.E.P	49.42%

Source of Finance

18.	Fixed Capital from Financial Institution	142.00
19.	Working Capital from Bank	73.13
20.	Self Raised Capital	59.87
	Total	275.00

Prior to venturing into this particular project, one should likely know the details of plant and machinery, raw materials details, for which the entrepreneurs should take advantage of Practical Project Execution Know How Report. This report can help you expedite the decision making at corporate level and in actual setting up the project

20

IMPORTED MACHINERY FOR CANDLE MAKING

Drawing process

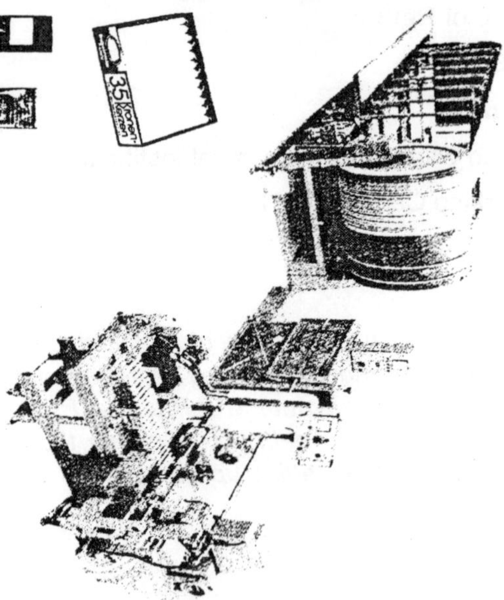

High-capacity continuous drawing system for the production of cylindrical candle Ø : 12-30 mm/L=70-430mm Output : up to11.000 candles/h.

System also available with integrated machines for taper candles, colour overdipping and automatic packaging.

Standard drawing system with manual finishing, suitable for candles up to 60 mm in dia and 1000 mm in length.

Candle Milling Machine

Candle Drawing Machine

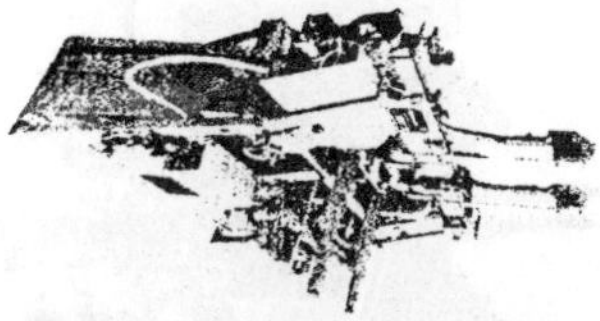

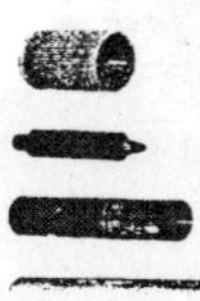

Milling and hot-die calibrating machine for pillar candles up to100mm ∅ manufactured from extruded candle strands produced out of white/solid coloured/ scented wax.

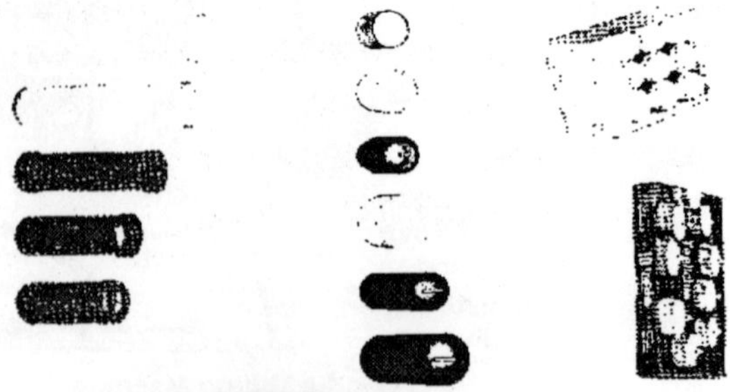

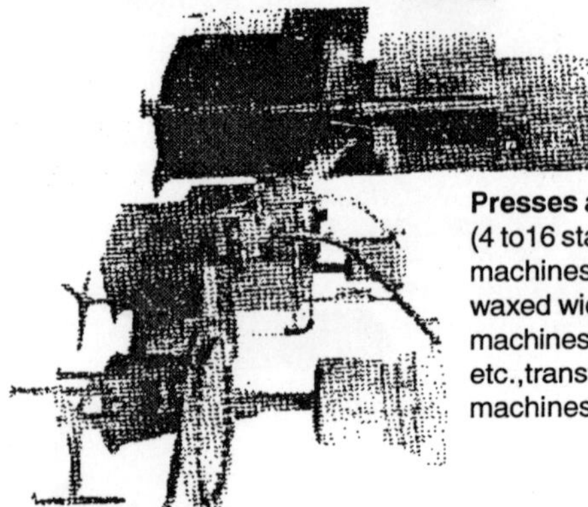

Presses available in different designs (4 to16 stamps) high capacity wicking machines for different kinds of pre-waxed wicks and sustainers,cupping machines for all sorts of cups/glasses etc.,transfer,labeling and packaging machines.

Drawing a wick through a liquid wax bath produces a candle strand which will be manufactured into candles by cutting/milling/melting etc.

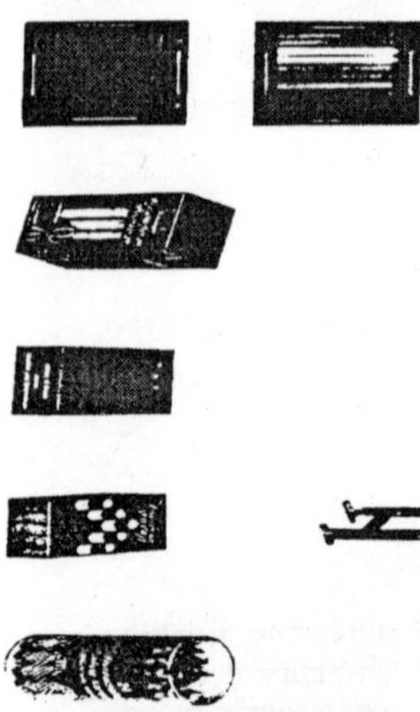

Machines for automatic packaging can be connected..

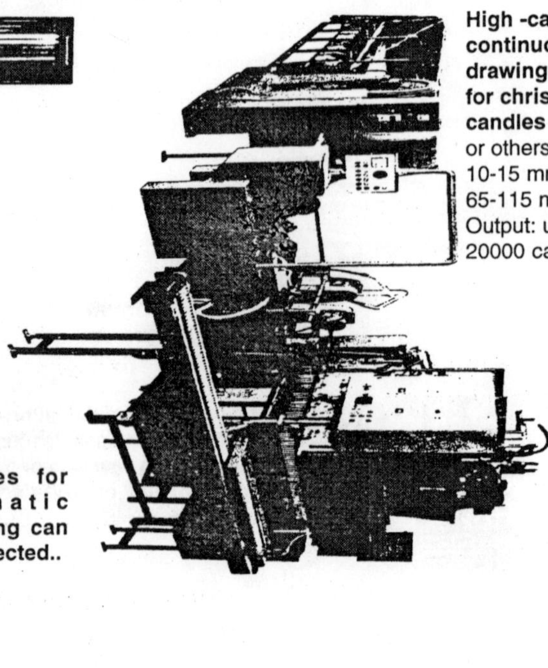

High -capacity continuous drawing system for christmas-tree-candles
or others 0 = 10-15 mm/l= 65-115 mm.
Output: up to 20000 candles/h

Continous birthday-candle drawing system
for candles up to 13 mm dia and 115 mm in length.Output:up to 16,000 candles per hour

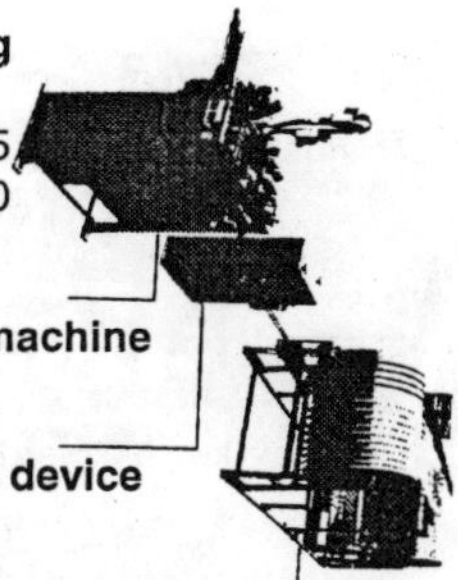

Milling machine

pull-out device

drawing machine

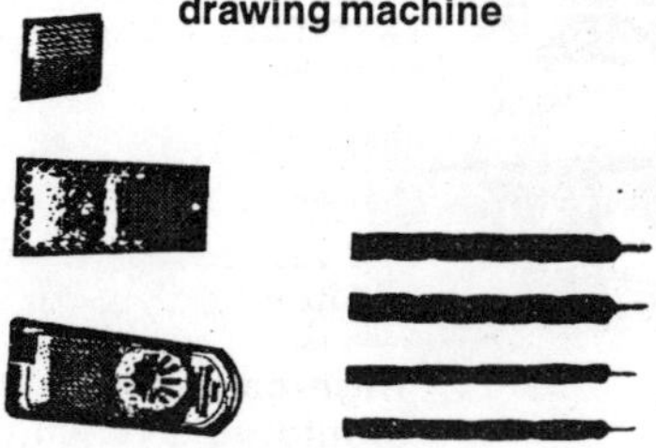

Extruding Process

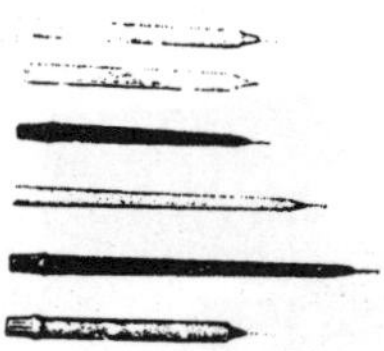

Piston extrution system with colour over dipping machine for the alternative production of cylindrical candles up to 11.000 pcs/h
Ø= 10-30 mm/L=70-430 mm
- tapered candles-up to 7.000 pcs/h
Ø =18-25 mm/l= 150-300 mm

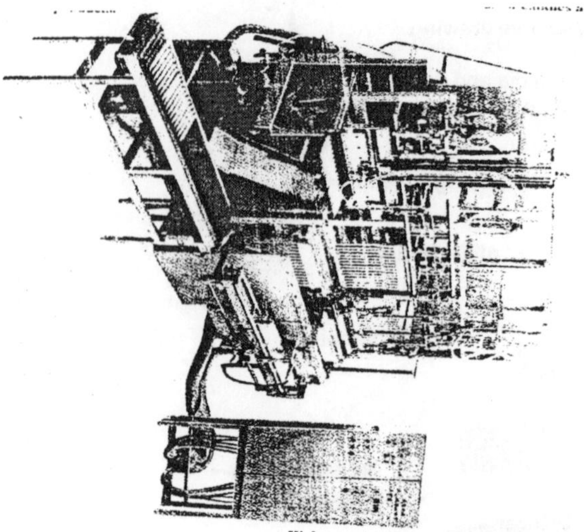

High-capacity universal moulding system, usable for different kinds of candles by simplest mould changing. Output:up to 4,500 candles/h

Dipping Process

Dipping plant for antique-finish tepered candles up to 650 mm length. Basic machine also usable for the production of flambeaus.

Production of candles and flambeaus by repeated dipping of wicks of flambeausticks in liquid wax

Accessory units for the candle dipping plant

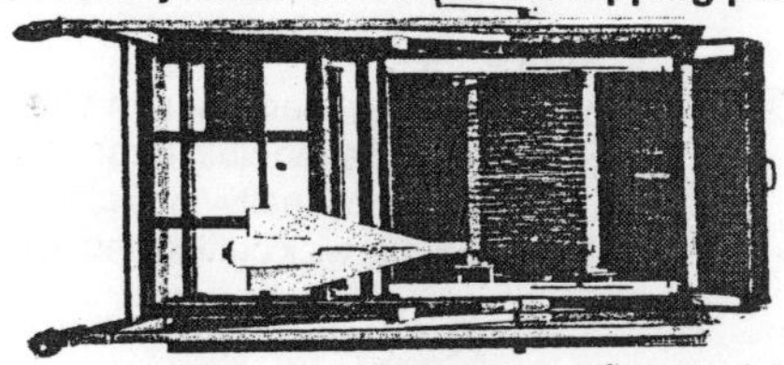

frame wicking device

transpor carriage with wicked frames and finished candles

colour overdipping machine

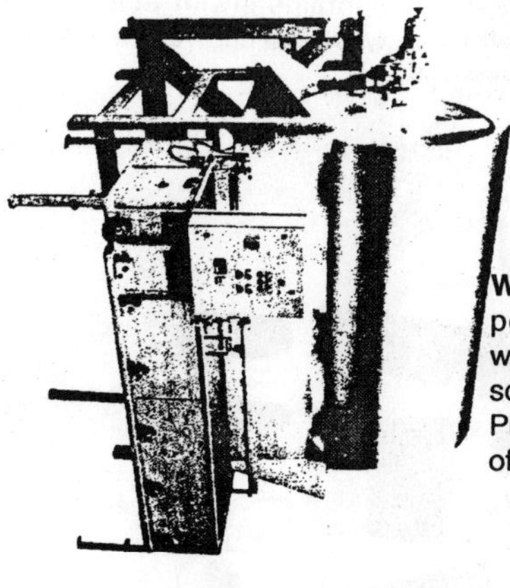

Wax spraying plants for powdering of all kinds of waxes,also solid coloured and scented.
Plants available for capacities of 300 up to 1,200kg/h

Moulding Process

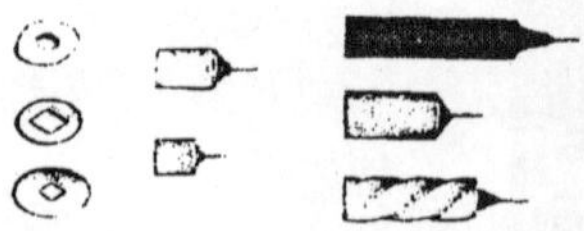

Candle moulding machines in standard and semi automatic designs,moulds arranged from 2 to 12 rows.Machines optionally available with motorized ejection,automatic wick cutting and overpour scraping.

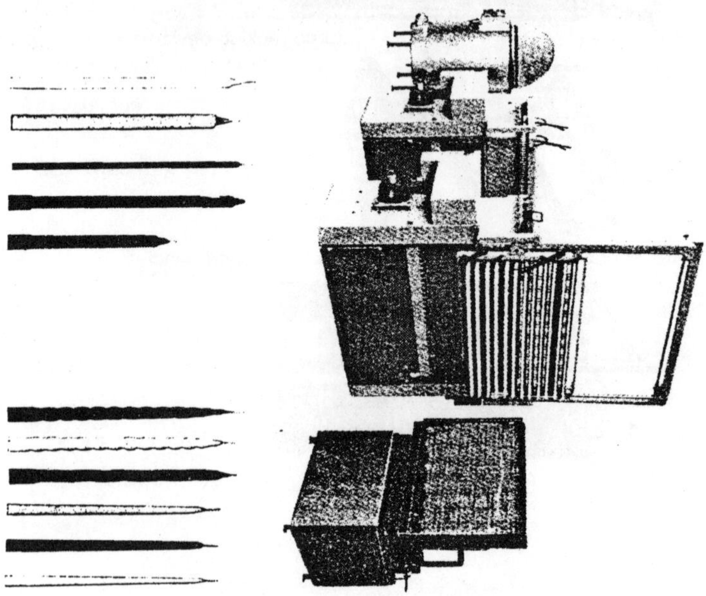

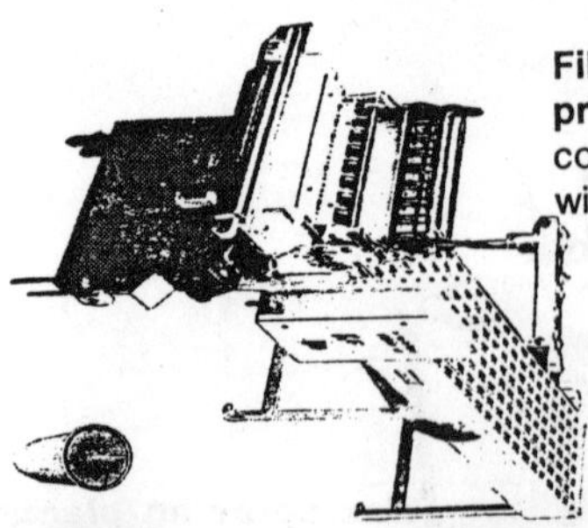

Filling plants for the fully automatic production of liquid filled candles in containers(with automatic centered wick) like cups/bottles/glasses etc.

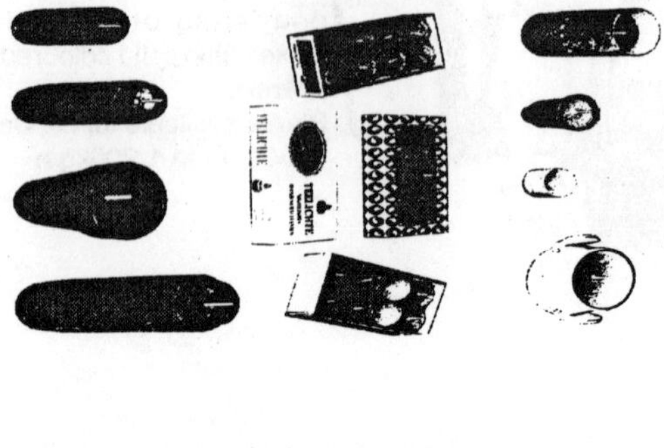

Packaging process

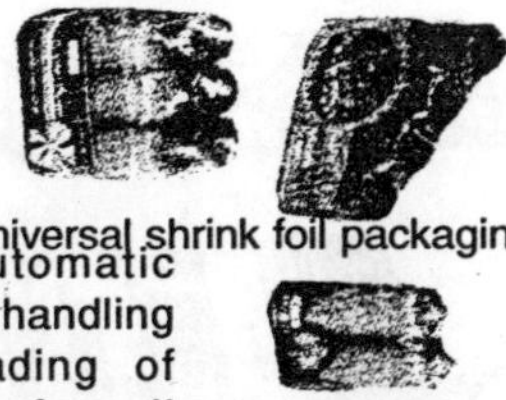

Universal shrink foil packaging systems

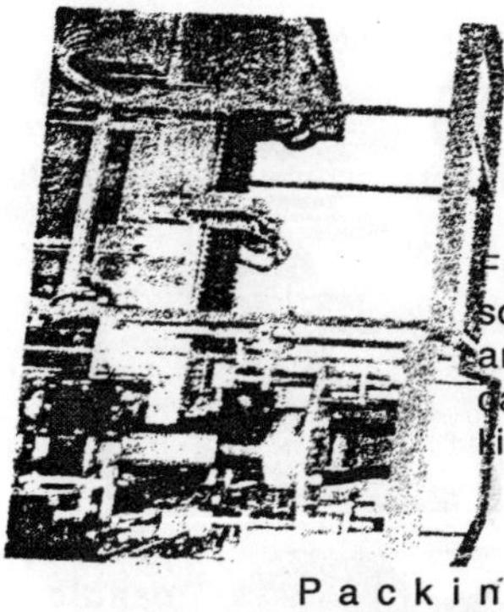

Fully-automatic sorting, handling and loading of candles for all kinds of packaging

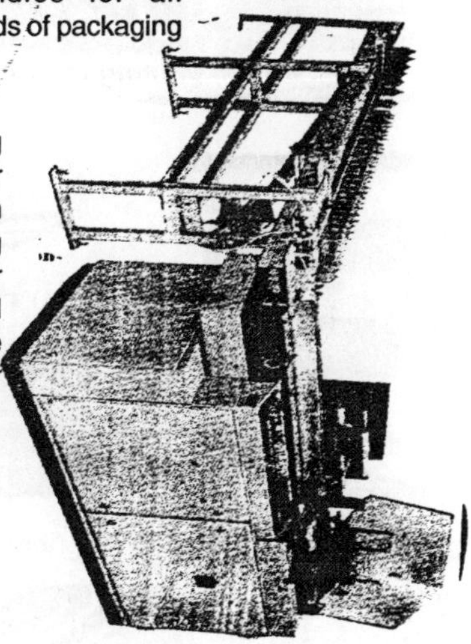

Packing machines for carton erecting,loading and closing for individual packings like trays,boxes or containers.

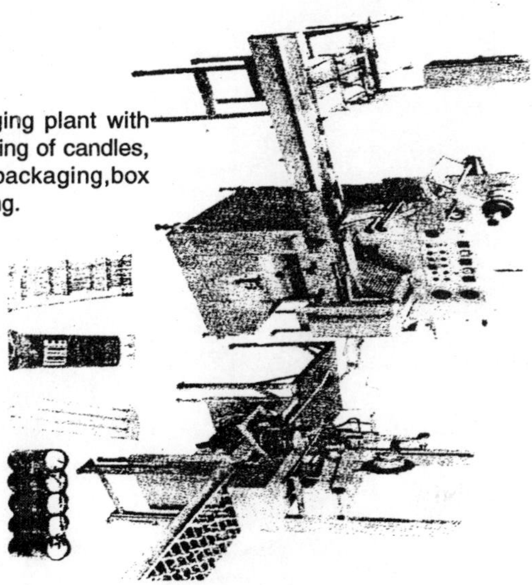

Complete packaging plant with handling and loading of candles, cellophane-bag-packaging,box closing and printing.

Finishing Process

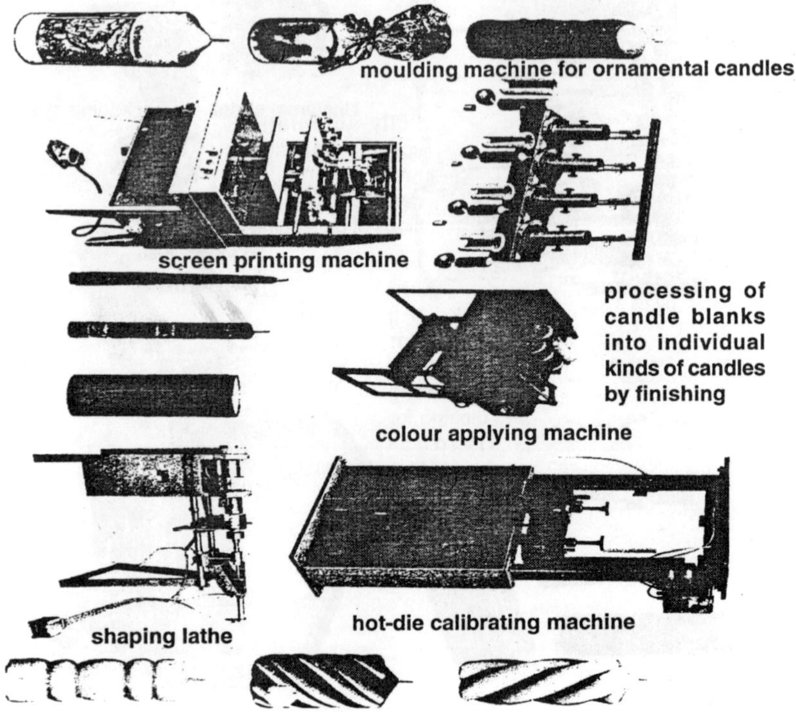

21

FAULTS

Listed here are some of the common problems likely to be encountered when making dipped and moulded candles, the probable reasons for them, and what best to do about them.

Dipping

Fault	*Cause*	*What To Do*
Lumpy surface on candle	First did too fast, Wax too cold whilst dipping.	Whilst candle is still warm, roll it on a smooth surface.
Candle spits whilst burning	Water in candle.	Pour off molten wax and relight candle. If this is not successful, then remelt it.
White marks in layers of dip and iron back candles	Wax too cold whilst dipping.	A quick dip in wax at 93°C (199°F) may be successful.
Candle cracks whilst plaiting or rolling	Uneven temperature throughout candle, i.e. the centre may be harder than the surface of the candle.	Re-dip candle until pliable.
Scum forms on the surface when floating wax on water	Impurities or dirty wax.	Ladle off scum. Make sure that you still have 3.8cm (1½in) of molten wax.
Damaged or old candle	Age, dirt, fading, etc.	Rub over surface with nylon stocking and white spirit. Decorate to cover flaws.

Casting in Moulds

Fault	*Cause*	*What To Do*
Air bubbles on surface	Poured too fast, Placed in water bath too soon. Dust in mould. Mould not tapped to remove air.	Pour slowly. Wait for one minute before placing in water bath. Clean mould. Tap mould one minute after pouring.

Seepage between candle and mould	Wax allowed to set and contract away from the side of the mould, allowing some of the topping-up wax to seep down the side.	Cutt off the unwanted marks.
Loss of definition with a layered candle	Previously poured wax not set sufficient to support the next layer. The surface should be rubbery.	Remelt. Remember that the resulting wax will be a combination of colours, usually brown.
Layers not joining	Wax poured too late or at too low a temperature.	Remelt.
Misshapen candle; sides caved in	Surface around wick not broken and probed soon enough. Air in centre of candle.	Keep surface constantly broken until candle is almost set.
Soap-like appearance	Too much stearin added.	Check proportion of wax mixture.
Candle will not come out of mould	Not enough stearin added. Candle topped up above the original level, causing seepage between candle and mould. Cooling too slow, resulting in insufficient contraction.	Place in hot water and melt candle out of mould. Alternatively, place in refrigerator for twenty minutes.
Ring of discolouration around top of candle	Dirty wax.	Take more care. Keep moulds and utensils clean.
Scaly marks on surface	Wax poured too cold for prevailing room temperature.	Use a water bath. Pour at a higher temperature.
Mould leaking from base	Careless wicking up. Damaged mould.	Seal with mould seal. Place candle in water bath immediately.
Small bubbly line encircling candle	Mark of water-level from water bath. Water added after candle placed in bath.	Rub with nylon stocking. Fill water bath almost to top of mould level before putting mould in.
Cracks throughout candle	Candle allowed to become too cold before topping.	Use water bath at room temperature.

22

COMMON SENSE WITH CANDLES

Fire Safety

Wax should be treated like cooking oil. At temperatures below 100°C (212°F) it is fairly safe and it will not catch fire. At higher temperatures wax starts to vaporize and is then liable to catch fire. The exact temperature depends upon the type of wax being used. It is best to treat all wax above 100°C (212°F) as though it were highly flammable. If wax does catch fire:

- Switch off the heat immediately. Do not move the pan.
- Do not try to put the fire out with water.
- Smother the flames with a damp cloth or metal lid.

Workshop Wisdom

Candlemaking is not an inherently messy occupation. This being said, upsets, minor and major, are bound to occur. However, with a little thought, most situations can be dealt with.

Prevention

• Wear old, comfortable clothes when making candles, and move or cover rugs and carpets. • Make sure that you have enough room in which to work, and that all your equipment and materials are readily to hand. • Remember that prolonged contact with hot molten wax will cause scalding. Do not leave pan handles sticking out from the cooker, and keep children and pets away from containers of hot wax. • Do not pour liquid wax down a sink or drain, as when it cools it will set and form a blockage.

Cure

• Spills or drips of wax should be allowed to cool and harden before tackling the problem. • For wax on clothing and carpets, scrape off what you can and then remove the residue by ironing through a sheet of absorbent paper (e.g. paper kitchen towel). Alternatively, you can send the item for dry-cleaning. • For wax on wood, scrape off the excess and then polish the residue with a soft cloth. • For wax on metal or plastic, immerse the item in hot water until the wax melts and floats to the surface. • White spirit or turpentine can be used to dissolve small amounts of cold wax.

23

CANDLE MAKING PLANT

Candle making unit is a profitable unit now-a-days as designed and perfumed candles are being exported to various other countries.

Since long, people used to burn cotton in mud cups filled with oil. In European countries previously people used to burn wooden sticks by dipping. These in facts due to the shortage of vegetable oils. About 25% of total population of India is living in villages where electricity was not available. But electricity is no problem these days, so kerosene oil lamps or wax candles are generally used for lighting purpose on special occasions. In the night or dark room, whenever electricity fails these candles play a big role in illuminating small and big cities, candles importance is also given in the encyclopedia of Britanica. In catholic church, candle was much preferred. The demand and consumption of candle is increasing day by day. In every village and town big and small grocer, general merchant, panwari, and perry shopkeepers sell candles. Paraffin wax was first time used in 1854. These days also candles are made of paraffin wax.

RAW MATERIALS

Imported plant is quite suitable to produce Perfumed and Designed Candles because Small/Cottage scale producers will not be the competitors as they shall not be in a position to invest this much amount.

Most modern candles are made from a mixture of several ingredients. They are paraffin wax, stearic acid, small quantities of other waxes being added usually for the sake of appearance. Probably this mixture which can be used in all method of making candles will prove most suitable for nearly all projects. However details of other materials which can be used are given below :

Paraffin wax is distilled from coal and oil shales and semi refined grades are used by most candle makers. It is usually supplied in the form of large blocks by petrol reining companies. For the several grades available the melting point is between 50° and 70°. For temperature climates 58°C melting point climate a higher melting point is necessary. Stearic Acid is a component of animal an vegetable fats and is supplied in flakes by oil and chemicals companies. It is added to wax to improve burning qualities and inc removing the finished candle from the mould easily. It also reduce the amount of smoke produced white burning. Between 5% and 50% of stearic acid can be used depending upon the quality of candle required on an average 10% is added. The more percentage of stearic acid the better the candle but the cost of the material should also be taken into account.

FORMULATION FOR CANDLES MAKING

1.	PARAFFIN WAX	60%
	STEARIC ACID	35%
	BEES WAX	5%
2.	PARAFFIN WAX	70 Parts
	STEARIC ACID	15 Parts
	PETROLEUM (OR ß-NAPHTHOL)	15 Parts
3.	PARAFFIN WAX	90 Parts
	STEARIC ACID	5 Parts
	PETROLEUM	5 Parts

CANDLES

1.	PARAFFIN WAX	40
	STEARIC ACID	20
	PARAFORMALDEHYDE	20
2.	PARAFFIN WAX	16
	STEARIC ACID	16
	PARAFORMALDEHYDE	8
	FORMALDEHYDE	5.5

Candles

Colouring Creasine Candles for the Christmas Tree. For coloring these candles only dye stuff, soluble in oil can be employed. Blue : 23-24 lavender blue, pale or dark, 100-120 parts per 5,000 parts of ceresine. Violet 26 fast violet R, 150 parts per 5,000 parts of ceresine. Silver gray : 29 silver gray, 150 parts per 5000 parts of ceresine. Yellow and orange : 30 wax yellow, medium, 200 parts per 5000 parts of ceresene; 61 old gold, 200 parts per

5000 ceresene. Pink and red : 27 peach-pink, or 29 chamois, about 100 parts per 5000 parts of ceresine. Green, 16-17, brilliant green, 33 may gre, 41 may green, 200-250 parts per 5000 parts of ceresene. The above named colors should be ground in oil and the ceresene tinted with them afterwards.

Plant Economics of Colour Flame Perfume Candle

Rated Plant Capacity	=	3000.00 Pkt/Day
LAND & BUILDING (Total Land 800 sq.mt)	=	Rented

PLANT & MACHINERY

1. Wax melting Pan made of iron and jacket for steam heating
2. Baby boiler
3. Semi Automatic Candle making machine
4. Colour making vessel made of mild steel
5. Other accessories

FIXED CAPITAL

1. PLANT & MACHINERY	Rs.	3,00,000.00
2. OTHER FIXED ASSETS	Rs.	93,000.00
TOTAL	Rs.	3,93,000.00

RAW MATERIALS

1. Paraffin wax
2. Cotton Wick
3. Colour Compound
4. Other perfumed materials like, musk ambrette, musk zylon, ciret, yara powder, red rose, bragomot oil,etc.
5. Packing material

TOTAL WORKING CAPITAL/ANNUM

1. RAW MATERIAL	Rs.	1,46,10,000.00
2. SALARY & WAGES	Rs.	5,50,620.00
3. UTILITIES & OVERHEADS	Rs.	3,94,300.00
TOTAL	Rs.	1,55,54,920.00

TOTAL CAPITAL INVESTMENT

TOTAL FIXED CAPITAL	Rs. 3,93,000.00
TOTAL WORKING CAPITAL FOR 1 MONTHS	Rs. 12,96,243.33
TOTAL	Rs. 16,89,243.33

TURN OVER/ANNUM

Receipt through sale of Packets 9,00,000 (each contain 12 candles)	Rs. 1,98,00,000.00

PROFIT SALES RATIO = PROFIT / SALES X 100 = 20.00 %

RATE OF RETURN = OPERATING PROFIT / T.C.I X 100 = 234.39 %

BREAK EVEN POINT (B.E.P) = 14.36 %

24

SMOKELESS CANDLE

Smokeless candle exhibit the speciality that they do not produce any black soat or carbon while burning and after burning.

It is by virtue of the special formulation and quality of wax. Even the wick is of special quality produced by dipping of wick in solution based on specific formulation.

Since long, people used to burn cotton in mud ups filled with oil. In European countries previously people used to burn wooden sticks by dipping. These in facts due to the shortage of vegetable oils. About 25% of total population of India is living in villages where electricity was not available. But electricity is no problem these days, so kerosene oil lamps or wax candles are generally used for lightning purpose on special occasions. In the night or dark room, wherever electricity fails these candles play a big role in illuminating small and big cities, candles play a big role in illuminating small and big cities, candles importance is also given in the encyclopedia of Britanica. In catholic church, candle was much preferred . The demand and consumption of candle is increasing day by day. In every village and town big and small grocer general merchant, panwari, and perry shopkeepers sell candles. Paraffin wax was first time used in 1854. These days also candles are made of paraffin wax.

Previously candles made by Burmah Oil Co. Ltd and Indo Burma Petroleum Industries were imported and in India candles were made out of stearin.

During world war II, import of candles was stopped and due to the shortage of kerosene oil candle making was given an added weightage. So many people in Calcutta started manufacturing candles in 1943, about 160 small scale factories were running in India for manufacturing candles, and at that time India was self sufficient in making candles and was also in a position to export candles. After 1947 due to shortage of paraffin wax is production of these candles was reduced. In 1949 production was 1200 tonnes only. Raw material for paraffin wax is being manufactured mainly by Sighoi refinery. The installed capacity for wax production has increased these days.

The candle industry uses as raw materials primarily the fatty acids which are produced from fats by hydrolysis and which are usually a mixture of two solid acids, the stearin (palmitic and stearic acids) and a liquid acid, olein (oleic acid). The separation of stearin and olein is the first task of he manufacturer of stearin, since only stearin can be processed to candles. This determines the selection of the raw material for the production of candles: Solid and semi-solid fats of animal or vegetable origin, such as beef tallow (inferior products), mutton tallow, bone fat fish tallow, fat wastes, palm oil, vegetable tallow. During the hydrolysis fats with H_2SO_4 catalyst, the acid reacts with liquid oleic acid so that the latter is converted,. after boiling with water, into a solid product (hydroxystearic acid), $C_{17}H_{34}OH.COOH$, and thus increases the solid fraction; for this reason, H_2SO_4 is used for the hydrolysis of fats in candle factories. However, the fatty acids obtained must be thoroughly freed from H_2SO_4 which is done by treatment with water vapor in leadlined containers.

FORMULATION OF SMOKELESS CANDLES

Ceresin Wax	60%
Stearin	15%
Bees Wax	15%
Stearic Acid	10%
TOTAL	100%

FORMULATION OF IMPORTED CANDLE WICKS

East German Patent	10,293
Benzene	50-70
Ethanol	30-50

Degrease wick with this mixture, then press and dry at 70°C. impregnate with sodium hydrogen phosphate (2% solution).

PROCESS OF MANUFACTURING OF SMOKELESS CANDLE

Process of Candle Moulding

Candles consist of cylinders of wax or fatty acids surrounding a wick lying true in the centre in order to avoid unequal burning. These wicks are made of cotton threads loosely plaited together and soaked in a solution of boric acid, potassium nitrate or chloride, and ammonium chloride, sulphate, or phosphate. The plaiting causes the wick to curve when burning, and thus they burn away at the ends without causing the flame to smoke. The chemical solution vitrifies the ash of the wick, and the minute glassy particles dropping off from the the bent wick leave the end free for the melted fat to ascend to the point where combustion is taking place. In the absence of this chemicals treatment the wick burns off short in the flame and causes persistent guttering. Stearine or paraffin candles are moulded in special machines.

It represents an ordinary candle machine capable of moulding ninety-six candles simultaneously. It consists of a battery of moulds contained in an iron tank A, through which warm or cold water can be passed as desired in order to heat or cool the moulds. Each mould is made of polished tin, sometimes backed by iron, and traversed by a piston which can be raised or lowered so as to force the candle out of the mould. The wicks are wound upon the bobbins D, and pass up the piston rods B accurately through the centres of the candle mouldsand end in a special clamp. To use the machine hot water is first driven through the box containing the moulds so as to heat them to a suitable temperature; next the melted wax is poured into the trough, and not only completely fills the moulds, but leaves a sufficient surplus in the troughs to allow for contraction of material on cooling. Next the hot water is replaced by a stream of cold, which rapidly chills the moulds, and the candles solidify. The wicks of the candles held in the clamp above the trough are now cut, and the previous round of candles carried away for packing. The excess of candle material in the trough is now removed by means of a suitable tool, the emptied clamp replaced over the trough, and then, by operating the handle, the pistons B are pushed up the moulds, thus forcing out the candles into the holder or clamp E. The wicks are drawn up with the candles, so that, immediately after the withdrawal of the first lot of candles, the pistons are lowered and another charge of wax poured into the moulds. When the surplus material in the trough is sufficiently solid, the wicks above are cut by a special knife or scissors, and the clamps containing the candles are then lifted away, and the candles ejected into a rack or other convenient place. After the clamps have been replaced upon the machine the operation is continued until, ultimately, the bobbins d, which contain sufficient wick for several hundreds of candles, are emptied, when they are either rewound or replaced by others.

PLANT ECONOMICS OF SMOKELESS CANDLES

Rated Plant Capacity	=	500.00 Kgs/Day
LAND & BUILDING (Land Area 300 sq. mts.)	=	Rs.5,00,000.00

PLANT & MACHINERY

1. Melting Pot of aluminium for wax with electric heaters
2. Candle moulds
3. Miscellaneous items,viz. water bath weighing scale, thermometer, pair of scissors, small ladle, tools, etc.

FIXED CAPITAL

1. LAND & BUILDING	Rs.	5,00,000.00
2. PLANT & MACHINERY	Rs.	1,35,000.00
3. OTHER FIXED ASSETS	Rs.	88,500.00
TOTAL	Rs.	7,23,500.00

RAW MATERIALS

1. Ceresin wax
2. Stearin
3. Bees wax
4. Stearic acid
5. Perfume like sandlewood camphor etc
6. Wicks
7. Packaging materials

TOTAL WORKING CAPITAL/MONTH

1. RAW MATERIAL	Rs.	6,49,750.00
2. SALARY & WAGES	Rs.	51,250.00
3. UTILITIES & OVERHEADS	Rs.	42,500.00
TOTAL	Rs.	7,43,500.00

TOTAL CAPITAL INVESTMENT

TOTAL FIXED CAPITAL	Rs.	7,23,500.00
TOTAL WORKING CAPITAL FOR 3 MONTHS	Rs.	22,30,500.00
TOTAL	Rs.	29,54,000.00

TURN OVER/ANNUM

By sale of 1,50,000 kgs. of candles Rs. 1,12,50,000.00

PROFIT SALES RATIO = PROFIT / SALES X 100 = 16.82 %

RATE OF RETURN = OPERATING PROFIT / T.C.I X 100 = 64.04 %

BREAK EVEN POINT (B.E.P) = 31.90 %

25

MOSQUITO REPELLENT CANDLE

Mosquito repellent candles are intended to repel mosquitoes even without being alighted.

These mosquitoes are one of the irritating pests which are carrying disease from person to person. These insects, owing to their prominence as disease carrying pests have probably received more alteration by scientists and workers than all other insects put together.

Repellents are materials that affect insects and other organisms and disrupt their natural behaviour.

Formulation	% age
Paraffin wax	5.5
Stearic acid	15
Petrolatum	15
Oil of citronella	7.50
Camphor	7.50
Pigments/dies	Q.S.
Total	100

PLANT ECONOMICS OF MOSQUITO REPELLENT CANDLES

Rated Plant Capacity = 500.00 Kgs/Day

LAND & BUILDING (Rented 3000/- per month.) = 3,000.00

PLANT & MACHINERY

1. Melting pot of aluminium for paraffin wax with electric heaters
2. Moulds (20 moulds each for 48 candles)
3. Miscellaneous items i.e. Weighing scale, tools, buckets etc.
4. Mixer agitator
5. Chiller with chilled water cooling arrangement

FIXED CAPITAL

1. LAND & BUILDING	Rs.	3,000.00
2. PLANT & MACHINERY	Rs.	1,45,000.00
3. OTHER FIXED ASSETS	Rs.	34,000.00
TOTAL	Rs.	1,82,000.00

RAW MATERIALS

1. Paraffin Wax
2. Stearic Acid
3. Petrolatum
4. Oil of Citronella
5. Comphor
6. Pigments/Dyes
7. Packing materials

TOTAL WORKING CAPITAL/MONTH

1. RAW MATERIAL	Rs.	8,38,125.00
2. SALARY & WAGES	Rs.	51,875.00
3. UTILITIES & OVERHEADS	Rs.	32,700.00
TOTAL	Rs.	9,22,700.00

TOTAL CAPITAL INVESTMENT

TOTAL FIXED CAPITAL	Rs.	1,82,000.00
TOTAL WORKING CAPITAL FOR 2 MONTHS	Rs.	18,45,400.00
TOTAL	Rs.	20,27,400.00

TURN OVER/ANNUM

By selling of 150,000 kg candle Rs.1,35,00,000.00

PROFIT SALES RATIO = Profit / Sales x 100 = 15.90 %

RATE OF RETURN = OPERATING PROFIT / T.C.I X 100 = 105.85 %

BREAK EVEN POINT (B.E.P) = 24.26 %

26

MAGIC CANDLE

The magic candles are covered in fire works industry. This type of candles may give multi coloured flame.

For starting the unit for Magic candles, following conditions have to be met essentially. This industry is covered under Indian explosive act and Rules 1940. The following licences are necessary before starting this industry.

1. A certificate from District Magistrate showing "No objection".
2. After getting the above certificate, an application has to be forwarded to the Area Inspector of Explosive seeking the permission to start the industry. The inspector will inspect the whole set up to ensure that the requirements are met as per rules and after satisfaction, approval will be obtained.

The following factors have also to be considered and necessary licences are required.

1. A licence from District Magistrate is required for storing and handling of sulphur.
2. A licence from State Chief Inspector of Factories is required under Indian Factories Rules.
3. A Municipal licence from Municipal commissioner is required to run the plant.
4. If personnel strength is 50 or more in electrically operated plant or 100 or more in hand operated plant, a licence from Ministry of Industries and Commerce, New Delhi, is required under Industrial Development Act, 1951.
5. Factory should be far away from the residential colony, railway line, and public roads etc.

Manufacturing Process of Magic Candle

Formulation of Colouring Compound for Magic Candle

Ingredients	*% age*
Potassium chloride	15
Strontium Nitrate	17
Potassium chlorote	5
Barium Nitrate	35
Sulphur	10
Clay	18
Total	100

Process

For the manufacture of colouring compound for magic candle of multi colour flame, all the ingredients are mixed in a mixer for proper mixing.

The above ingredients are to be obtained in fine mesh powder. The mixing process may also be done by hand, as not much quantity is required.

This colouring compound for magic candle is now mixed in a paraffin wax at the time of wax melting for making magic candle.

The candle while burning gives a multicolour flame and it is very appealing.

Formulation of Magic Candle	**Parts/wt.**
Paraffin wax	67
Stearic Acid	30
Colouring Compound for multi colour flame	3
Total	100

PLANT ECONOMICS OF MAGIC CANDLES

Rated Plant Capacity	=	500.00 Kg/Day
LAND & BUILDING (Land Area 400 sq.mt)	=	Rs. 8,80,000.00

PLANT & MACHINERY

1. Wax melting pan made of iron and jacket for steam heating
2. Baby boiler
3. Semi Automatic Candle making machine
4. Colour making vessel made of mild steel
5. Other accessories

FIXED CAPITAL

1. LAND & BUILDING	Rs.	8,80,000.00
2. PLANT & MACHINERY	Rs.	1,90,000.00
3. OTHER FIXED ASSETS	Rs.	60,000.00
TOTAL	Rs.	11,30,000.00

RAW MATERIALS

1. Paraffin wax
2. Stearic Acid
3. Misc. Colouring compound, cotton wicks and other consumables.
4. Packaging Materials

TOTAL WORKING CAPITAL/MONTH

1. RAW MATERIAL	Rs.	4,76,700.00
2. SALARY & WAGES	Rs.	40,000.00
3. UTILITIES & OVERHEADS	Rs.	39,700.00
TOTAL	Rs.	5,56,400.00

TOTAL CAPITAL INVESTMENT

TOTAL FIXED CAPITAL	Rs.	11,30,000.00
TOTAL WORKING CAPITAL FOR 2 MONTHS	Rs.	11,12,800.00
TOTAL	Rs.	22,42,800.00

TURN OVER/ANNUM

Receipt through sale of 150000 kgs. of Magic candles	Rs.	90,00,000.00

PROFIT SALES RATIO = PROFIT / SALES X 100 = 21.48 %

RATE OF RETURN = OPERATING PROFIT / T.C.I X 100 = 86.21 %

BREAK EVEN POINT (B.E.P) = 28.54 %

27

COLOURED FLAME CANDLES (RED, BLUE & GREEN FLAME)

The colour candles are covered in Fire works industry. This type of candles may give any coloured flame depending upon the formulation. Generally, the candles which give red, blue and green flames have been discussed in this report.

For starting the unit for coloured candles, following conditions have to be met essentially. This industry is covered under Indian explosive act and Rules 1940. The following licences are necessary before starting this industry.

1. A certificate from District Magistrate showing "No objection".
2. After getting the above certificate, an application has to be forwarded to the Area Inspector of Explosive seeking the permission to start the industry. The inspector will inspect the whole set up to ensure that the requirements are met as per rules and after satisfaction, approval will be obtained.

The following factors have also to be considered and necessary licences are required.

1. A licence from District Magistrateis required for storing and handling of sulphur.
2. A licence from State Chief Inspector of Factories is required under Indian Factories Rules.
3. A Municipal licence from Municipal commissioner is required to run the plant.
4. If personnel strength is 50 or more in electrically operated plant or 100 or more in hand operated plant, a licence from Ministry of Industries and Commerce, New Delhi, is required under Industrial Development Act, 1951.

5. Factory should be far away from the residential colony, railway line, and public roads etc.

During the beginning of Nineteenth century, the survey and experiments on animal fats and oils concluded that fats and oils are made of two ingredients fatty acid and glycerine. Immediately they invented a process in which it could have been possible to saponify and separated both these ingredients. By virtue of development of this process, solid stearin or stearic acid is available in India in sufficient quantity.

The candles were also first prepared from this stearin and the performance of the candles was quite satisfactory but the cost was on higher side. Later, the stearin was substituted with paraffin wax.

Now a days paraffin wax is also in short supply and available from government quota only. Some people are selling parraffin wax at premium.

PERFUMED CANDLES

Introduction

Candles made of wax are well known amongst every person of the world, but perfumed candle is a new type of candle which apart from providing light should also give perfumes. It serves two purpose in one purpose it acts as candle and in another as incense stick or dhoop batti.

Perfumed candles are some what costlier than ordinary type candles and this is the reason they are not being manufactured in India so far. Another reason for not being manufactured in that candles are available easily for lighting purposes and agarbatti and dhoopbatti for perfumes. There are very little cases, where both the things are required simultaneously and if happens so, candles and other perfumed articles are used.

Almost all type of candles whether ordinary or perfumed have the basic raw material paraffin wax. During the beginning of 19th century, some scientists conducted the survey and experiments on animal fats and oil and calculated that fats and oils are made of two ingredients fatty acid and glycerine. Immediately they invented a process in which it could have been possible to saponify and separated both these ingredients. By virtue of development of this process, solid stearin or stearic acid is available in India in sufficient quantity.

The candles were also first prepared from this stearin and the performance of the candles was quite satisfactory but the cost was on higher side. Later, the stearin was substituted with paraffin wax.

Now a days paraffin was is also in short suppply and available from government quota only. Some people are selling parraffin wax at premium.

MANUFACTURING PROCESS (COLOURED)

The colour candles manufacturing has been divided into the following:

1. Making of compound for different colour flame.
2. Mixing of the compound into the wax.
3. Candle making.

1. Compound Machine

First of all the compound of desired colour flame is prepared the following are different formulations.

a) For Red Colour

Potassium Chloride	40%
Storontium Nitrate	35%
Sulphur	10%
Clay	15%
Total	100%

b) For Green Colour:

Potassium Chlorate	28%
Barium Nitrate	60%
Sulphur	12%

c) For Blue Colour

Potassium Chlorate	32%
Barium Nitrate	28%
Sulphur	18%
Clay	22%

The above chemicals are to be obtained in fine mesh powder mixing and mixed together properly. The mixing process may be done by hand also as no much quantity is required.

Plant & Machinery Suppliers (INDIAN)

Vinod Industries
Lal Kuan, Delhi - 110 006
Ph : 23217969, 23212602
Mr. Vinod Bhalla

Vijay Industries
1787, Lal Kuan,
Delhi - 110 006
Ph : 23951942, 23950195

PLANT ECONOMICS OF COLOURED FLAME CANDLES (RED, BLUE & GREEN FLAME)

Rated Plant Capacity = 3000.00 Pkt/Day

LAND & BUILDING (Land Area 500 sq.mt) = Rs.14,35,000.00

PLANT & MACHINERY

1. Wax melting Pan made of iron and jacket for steam heating
2. Baby boiler
3. Semi Automatic Candle making machine
4. Colour making vessel made of mild steel
5. Other accessories

FIXED CAPITAL

1. LAND & BUILDING	Rs. 14,35,000.00
2. PLANT & MACHINERY	Rs. 2,80,000.00
3. OTHER FIXED ASSETS	Rs. 70,500.00
TOTAL	Rs. 17,85,500.00

RAW MATERIALS

1. Paraffin wax
2. Cotton Wick
3. Colour Compound
4. Other perfumed materials like, musk ambrette, musk zylon, ciret, yara powder, red rose, bragomot oil,etc
5. Packing material

TOTAL WORKING CAPITAL/ANNUM

1. RAW MATERIAL	Rs. 97,15,000.00
2. SALARY & WAGES	Rs. 4,73,800.00
3. UTILITIES & OVERHEADS	Rs. 2,06,000.00
TOTAL	Rs.1,03,94,800.00

TOTAL CAPITAL INVESTMENT

TOTAL FIXED CAPITAL	Rs. 17,85,500.00
TOTAL WORKING CAPITAL FOR 2 MONTHS	Rs. 17,32,466.67
TOTAL	Rs. 35,17,966.67

TURN OVER/ANNUM

Receipt through sale of 9,00,000 Pkts (each contain 12 candles)	Rs. 1,80,00,000.00

PROFIT SALES RATIO = PROFIT / SALES X 100 = 38.89 %

RATE OF RETURN = OPERATING PROFIT / T.C.I X 100 = 198.97 %

BREAK EVEN POINT (B.E.P) = 11.14 %

28

CANDLE MAKING UNIT (SEMI AUTOMATIC)

Candles of different sizes, colour and designs can be manufactured for higher sales. Candles play great importance and are used mainly on festivals like Deepawali and Christmas. Candles in huge amount are sold mainly in festivals for illumination purposes. People use candles of different design and shapes as decoration pieces.

These are also widely used in villages where people face shortage of electricity and are also used in cities for lighting during electricity shortage or break down period. Artistic candles find use in big hotels, restaurants, clubs, churches and kothies & Bunglows inspite of their high cost. These candles are of a good quality and finish and give very good flame. This type of candles does not bend also at the time of burning and therefore preferred.

It is more beneficial to make artistic candles than making ordinary candles for greater market in big cities but for smaller cities and villages, ordinary and improved quality of candles are of great use even and to an ordinary man as well as rich persons.

MANUFACTURING PROCESS

Candle Making Techniques

There are 4 methods of producing candles on a small scale of production. These are outlined briefly, then described at greater length.

The Dipping Process. This techinique consists of immersing the candle wick in molten wax then withdrawing it, so that it picks up wax as it emerges. The wax is allowed to cool and the process is repeated until the required thickness has been built up. The equipment is very simple in principle and can also be simply made.

The Pouring Process. This technique consists of suspending a wick over a container of melted wax and pouring hot wax and pouting hot wax from a small ladle so that it runs down the wick, colling as it goes. Any surplus wax drips back into the main container, and can be used again. In terms of equipment this is the simplest method. To produce good candles in this way a fair degree of skill must be acquired.

The Moulding or Casting Process. The moulding technique consists of filling a mould, in which a wick has been positioned with melted wax, allowing the wax to cool and then removing the completed candle from the mould. Except for very small output per day, a certain degree of sophistication in mould design and fairly large numbers of moulds are needed. Machines for casting candles in large numbers are avaialble, and as they do not require power for operation, a description of them is included.

The Drawing Process. A long length of wick is passed back and forth horizontally through a bath of wax, forming a candle 'rope', which is accommodated on large drums which are manually operated. The 'rope' is then cut into candle lengths. A mechanised version of this machine does give much higher output, but at greatly increased capital cost.

The Dipping Process

Candle dipping offers a method of producing several hundred candles a day with relatively simple equipment. The candles may be 30 cm long or considerbly more, in which case they can be cut as described in the section on the drawing process. Diameter can be up to 10 cm or even more.

A number of wicks are suspended and repeately dipped into wax to build up candles in successive layers round the wicks. Excess wax drains off, but some remains at the lower end, which is therefore thicker. For this reason candles made in this way are often called tapers. However, with correct dipping technique and by discarding the lower 10 cm or so, uniform diameter candles can be produced.

The equipment for dipping can range from a stick from which the candles are suspended wax and withdrawn as smoothly as possible, so that the wax deposits are even layers with no drips or surface imperfections.

To obtain a well formed candle, the candle wick should be submerged in the melted wax and withdrawn as smoothly as possible, so that the wax deposits are even layers with no drips or surface imperfections.

Using this technique a semi-refined paraffin wax with a melting point of 54°C (130° F) is required. To this 20 per cent of stearic acid should be added. The addition of about 5 per cent beeswax will improve the qualities of adhesion of the wax. Do not use micro-crystalline wax, as this tends to deposit at a faster rate thean other waxes and may prevent adhesion from occurring naturally.

The paraffin wax should be broken into piecs of a convenient size, weighted to the required quantity and placed in the vat (container). Add to it the right quantity of stearic acid or stearline, and the beeswax if required. Heat gently until all the contents have melted and blended together. When the occurs, allows the blend to cool to about 49°C (120°F) before attempting to dip. It is advisable to experiment with various temperatures to find the one which suits the blend best. It is important that a sufficient quantity and depth of melted wax is maintained in the container at all times.

A can or wax-pot deeper than the length of the longest candle to be made is required, with sufficient height about the wax level to allow for displacement of the wax. It can be heated by any one of several methods described later, but as the wax is to be kept at a constant temperature for a considerable time and is cooled by immersion of the candles, continuous heating, insulation and, ideally, thermostatic controls are advantageous.

The wax used is 90 per cent paraffin with a melting point of 58°C, and 10 per cent sterline. Wicks for candles up to 3 cm are 15 ply braided.

The wicks are tied to the dipping frames and weighted at their lower ends. The wax is heated to 75°C and the first group of wicks lowered into it. They should be left to soak for 3 minutes to allow air and moisture to escape; this should be done with each new group of wicks. The pre-waxed wicked should be drawn through the fingers as they cool, to smooth off any lumps. This will ensure that the final candles are smooth and uniform.

When all the wicks have been pre-waxed, the dipping proper begins. Each dip should be carried out slowly and smoothly, leaving the candle immersed for 5 to 10 seconds. The groups of candles are worked round in turn, and the time between dips for each group should be between 2 and 5 minutes.

For practical production, conditions should be such as to give the best appearance to the candles with the least number of dips. Various factors affect the performance :

Increasing time between dips reduces the number of dips needed.

Increasing wax temperature increases the number of dips needed.

Higher air temperature increases the time needed between dips-to compensate reduce the air temperature.

Dipping

A simple stand and boiler suitable for dipping candles. The wick holder is made of wood and holds approximately 12 wicks. The wick holder is placed in a jig which is slid up and down on guides, thus immersing the wicks each time until the required thickness of candle is achieved. The wick holder is then removed and another one inserted. A continuous dipping process for four or more wick holders. The production rate from this machine will obviously be much greater that that from the single wick holder.

Finally, the candles are removed, trimmed at their lower ends and allowed to cool. They may be rooled in the same way as poured candled. An alternative and convenient methods of removing the weights is to dip the ends in hot wax, then cut the wicks.

The Pouring Process

The wax is heated to a temperature of 75°C and using the ladle, wax is poured down each wick in turn, the wax failling off the wicks going back into the melter. It is also possible to have the excess wax fall into a separate can. As can pouring is made, the wheel is turned. During pouring the wick should be twisted slowely, which helps to form an even coating. The process is continued until the desired thickness of wax is built up.

Only a certain amount of wax can be added at each time of pouring; the wax is therefore built up in layers and extremes must be avoided. If the candles are too warm and the wax is also hot, one pouring will tend to melt the previous one off. So, the temperature of the wax may have to be adjusted according to the speed of working round the wheel, the workshop temperature and also for the exact composition of the wax.

During pouring candles may sway a bit and stick togeather, If the happends, they can be gently separated with a knife or by tapping.

When sufficient thickness has been built up, the can dles are removed from the wheel and the bottom ends with the weights cut off. They can then be rolled smooth on a warm glass, metal or stone slab, after which they should be hung of their wicks for 24 hours to cool.

The blend of wax required for the technique is the same as that used for the dipping methods i.e. a mimxture of 90 per cent paraffin wax of 58% C melting point and 10 per cent stearline is used. For church use a proportion of beeswax might be reuired through this adds considerably to the cost.

Pouring

This rig consists of an old cycle wheel in a horizontal plane supported by a vertical shaft, the length of which is determined by a suitable working position. The bottom end of the shaft for working. Thw wheel must be able to rotate freely. Small metalhooks made approximately 3mm diameter wire are fixed to the outer rim of the wheel, from which the candle wicks are suspended and kept rigid in a vertical position using small lead weights at the borrom of each wick. A heated container, similar to that used in the previous technique, is positioned so that the outer rim of the wheel is above the centre of the container. A small ladle is required for pouring the heated wax over the wick.

The Moulding or Casting Process

Casting (or moulding) is most suitable for the following conditions :

- For a household making candles only for its own use, so that the number required is very small.
- For candles which are decorative rather than strictly utilitarian, in which many techniques of colouring, texturing and the production of special shapes are used, and for candles over 4cm in diameter.
- In mass production of plain candles, in which case special machines are used.

Thus casting is not really suitable for use on a small industry basis if plain candles are to be produced. The techncial reasons are that moulds must be really well designed and accurately made if they are to be reliable, that continual during cooling is needed for topping up as the wax contracts, and that for a comparable output to say, candle-drawing, a large number of moulds is needed. How ever, the methods can produce highly finished and decorative candles.

The technique is again very simple. It consists of suspending a wick in a mould (tied to a rod at the top), and then filling the cavity of the mould with molten wax. When the wax has cooled and set, the finished candle can be removed from the mould and will be an exact replica of the inside shape of the mould. One advantage of using this method is that it requires very little work to be done, once the candle of removed from the mould. The wax in the mould must be allowed to cool slowly. As the wax cools it shrinks, so add a little more wax every so often, just to keep the top more or less level. When the candle has completely set, it should be possible to lift it out of the mould without any trouble. If the candle does tend to bind in the mould, it is likely that the wax and temperature used were not correct for this method.

A hard wax is required for casting, as it is less likely to adhere to the mould. As hardness can be gauged by a high melting point, wax which melts in the region of 60°C to 68°C (140°F-155°F) is required. The temperature for filling a mould should not be lower than 80°C (175°F) and not higher than 88°C (190°F).

A good basic paraffin wax should be selected for moulding. It should be hard, and requires a high melting point, at the temperatures previously mentioned. A relateively high percentage of stearic acid, between 10 and 30 per cent, should be added, and to obtain a good surface finish resistant to abrasion and dust penetration, 3 per cent of micro-crystalline wax is necessary. This will also ensure a good clean release from the mould,as it is too hard to adhere. This blend will produce a high quality, long-burning candle.

A perfectly adequate simple candle can be made using nothing other than paraffin wax, which could be sufficient, depending on the market demand. As the wax in the mould cools, each candle should be probed with a long thin rod and 'opened'. If a hole is seen, this should be filed with fresh wax. The process may have to be repeated until all the wax has solidified. During solidification , wax contracts by 20 per cent so that if this procedure is not followed there are likely to be holes in the candles, particularly in the region of the wick.

Once the wax is solid, but not yet cool, the mould can be immersed in water-if in running water, cooling is much quicker. When the wax is cool the wicks can be taken off the top metal bat(s) and the candles can be pushed out of the moulds by pressing the bottom plugs or burngs through.

If there are persistent problems of release, the following can be tried:

Increase the propertion of stearline

Tin-plate the inside of the mould tubes

Spray the inside of the moulds with silicone (expensive)

Moulding

The illustration shows a bench, boiler and moulds required for this method. The reason why only rough dimensions are shown on these sketches is because it is felt that these requirements are best left to those who are able to assess the most suitable size of the bench and moulds togeather with the number that meets their own individual output requirements. A more modest design of a set of moulds is shown.

The bench can be of wood construction, but it is suggested that the main surface should be covered with a layer of thin metal sheet. This ensures easier cleaning of any sulpus wax that may overflow from the moulds whilst pouring. The reason why the top section of the bench is divided into small square boxes is to ensure that the moulds remain in an upright steady position, thus avoding any accidental overturning of the moulds whilst the pouring action is in progress. The position of the wax boiler is not necessary where shown, but should be located in a convenient position to ensure easy access to the wax.

The mould is made from a metal seamless pipe, but any suitable container can be used, providing the inside is smooth and parallel, thus ensuring easy removal of the candle when completed. The metal bung at the base of the mould gives a suitable shape to the top of the finished candle, but it could also serve another purpose - it can be pushed in an upward direction, thus assisting in the removal of the finished candle without damage. The small metal bar at the top of the mould is for supporting the candle wick.

The Candle Drawing Method

A large number of candles can be produced by this method. It requires a simple machine which can be made by craftsmen, but is also commercially (from Arthur Weissbach, Fulda, W.Germany). However the Weissbach machine (and presumably those from other firms) is arranged for steam heating,s so would have to be adapted. Candles up to 6cm diameter can be made, but 3cm is a more practical limit.

The technique requires three people to operate it, and some skill has to be acquired. This should not present a seious problem.

Wax at a temperature of 75°C is used, with a ten per cent stearine content. Wicks for candle up to 3cm are 15 ply braided.

A 'rope' of candle is produced by drawing the wick through the through of wax. The first pass should be rather slow to ensure that all air escapes from the wick. As the wick emerges from the trough, it should be smoothed with the fingers, or, if this is found to be uncomfortable, a piece of thick felt or any other convenient device can be used.

After the first pass through the through the direction of winding th drums is reversed, so that the wick picks up another layer of wax and so on until the waxed rope exactly fits the sizing ring.

Sucess with this machine depends on keeping the rope warm enough to remain flexible, so that the workshop must be at a temperature of at least 25°C. This makes the technique particularly suitable for tropical climates. In cooler areas the workshop must be heated.

When the rope is complete it must be cut into candle lengths. Machines are available for this; however the job can be done by ahdn. The rope is led on to a cutting table of any smooth and hard material, and cut into lengths with a sharp knife. This is not difficult while the wax is still fairly soft. Then about 1cm of wick must be exposed at one end of each candle. Using a knife with a rolling rather than a downward cutting action, the wax can be cut, without at the same time cutting the wick, and the butt of the wax removed. The knack is soon picked up. In practice, cutting to length and exposing the wick are done at the same time.

If desired, the wick ends of the candles can then be tapered. To do this by hand, the end is rolled at an angle on a hard surface. However, this is not strictly necessary for utilitarian candles, though it doe improve the appearance of the candle.

Drawing

The wick is first coiled on a large drum about 120cm in diameter and 60cm wide, mounted with its axle horszontal and fitted with a handle for turning. It then passes through a heated trough containing wax. this trough should be about 150cm long, 40cm wide and 14cm deep. At the end of the trough is a sizing gauge, consisting of a ring of steel (or hardwood) With a series of varying size holes drilled through it, the wick being passed through one of the holes which controls the finished size of the candles. Finally the wick is led on to a second drum similar to the first.

Methods of Melting the Wax

All methods of making candles naturally start with melting the wax. The equipment for melting depends, of course, on what source of heat is available. The safety aspect must be considered before anything else. Wax must no be overheated, but the safety margin as far as fire risk is concered is wide, since molten wax has a reasonable high flash point. However, wax should be heated above 150°C as at high temperatures unpleasant and dangerous fumes are given off. This temperature is well above any needed in candle making but the woekshop should always be well ventilated.

Naturally, any wax split onto a naked flame or onto a red-hot electric heater will catch fire immediately, and a large-scale fire is then very likely. So although these heaters can be used, precautions must be taken against this kind of accident.

Heating Equipment

Electricity : Ideal for small and medium size woekshops, if available. Tanks or melting pots can be placed on 'Black heat'type heaters, or heating elements can be bolted to the bottom of a tank. Immersion heaters are not suitable.

Gas : Tanks or pots placed on gas heaters can be used providing the borrom is thack enough to prevent burning the wax. Asbestos mats can be used under the pot, but they need looking at regularly,as their life-span is not great. The warning about naked flames, of course, applies here.

Small quantities of wax as used, for example, in the pouring technique - can be melted in a gas-heated water jacket. Melting is rather slow, but the wax will be held at the right temperature for some time. However, care must be taken not to let the water boil away, and as this is very liable to happen, water jacket are not always considered ideal.

Solid fuel : Where no other fuel is available, melting pots can be placed on a specially constructed or possibly a standard type oven can be built from fireproof bricks.

Steam In large installations steam heating is used, the steam being led into double-walled heating pots. No attempt should be made to construct steam heating plant unless proper engineering facilities are available.

For all four methods, wax pots and tanks must be leak proof (not soldered) and should be of steel, iron or aluminium. Copper and brass should be avoided, as they cause oxidation.

Thermometers

It is possible to make candles without a thermometer, but the operation tends to be 'hit or miss;. Fortunately, thermometers are not very expensive and several types can be used. In all cases a range of up to 100°C is needed.

Types available include an ordinary mercury in glass, reading up to 100°C, which is very cheap; secondly a sugar thermometer, normally in domestic use for bottling, jam-making etc; thirdly a commercial rotary-type all-metal thermometer, which tends to be rather more expensive; and lastly three is the remote dial or washing machine-type thermometer; where the bulb is fixed into the tank and the dial mounted on a convenient bracket nearby-this is an expensive thermometer.

PLANT ECONOMICS OF CANDLE MAKING UNIT (SEMI AUTOMATIC)

Rated Plant Capacity	=	600.00 Kgs/Day
LAND & BUILDING (Land Area 300 sq.mts.)	=	Rs. 2,60,000.00

PLANT & MACHINERY

1. Candle Making machine
2. Additional accessories for above such as Bobbin winding attachment.
3. Melting vessel
4. Heating Arrangment oil fired or gas fired
5. Automatic Candles Packing machine
6. Sieves various sizes

FIXED CAPITAL

1. LAND & BUILDING	Rs.	2,60,000.00
2. PLANT & MACHINERY	Rs.	44,000.00
3. OTHER FIXED ASSETS	Rs.	55,000.00
TOTAL	Rs.	3,59,000.00

RAW MATERIALS

1. Hard Paraffin Wax
2. Stearic acid
3. Beeswax
4. Perfume wax like camphor or sandlewood
5. Wicks

TOTAL WORKING CAPITAL/MONTH

1. RAW MATERIAL	Rs.	4,03,600.00
2. SALARY & WAGES	Rs.	18,600.00
3. UTILITIES & OVERHEADS	Rs.	14,500.00
TOTAL	Rs.	4,36,700.00

TOTAL CAPITAL INVESTMENT

TOTAL FIXED CAPITAL	Rs.	3,59,000.00
TOTAL WORKING CAPITAL FOR 3 MONTHS	Rs.	13,10,100.00
TOTAL	Rs.	16,69,100.00

TURN OVER/ANNUM

1. Receipts for Sale of 15mm dia. Candles 45,000 Kgs.
2. Receipts from Sale of 25mm dia. Candles 1,35,000 Kgs.

TOTAL Rs. 72,00,000.00

PROFIT SALES RATIO = PROFIT / SALES X 100 = 23.06 %

RATE OF RETURN = OPERATING PROFIT / T.C.I X 100 = 99.47 %

BREAK EVEN POINT (B.E.P) = 21.63 %

29

CANDLE MAKING (NON -DRIP)

Since long, people used to burn cotton in mud ups filled with oil. In European countries previously people used to burn wooden sticks by dipping. These in facts due to the shortage of vegetable oils. About 25% of total population of India is living in villages where electricity was not available. But electricity is no problem these days, so kerosene oil lamps or wax candles are generally used for lightning purpose on special occasions. In the night or dark room, wherever electricity fails these candles play a big role in illuminating small and big cities,candles play a big role in illuminating small and big cities, candles importance is also given in the encyclopaedia of Britanica. In catholic church, candle was much preferred . The demand and consumption of candle is increasing day by day. In every village and town big and small grocer general merchant, panwari, and perry shopkeepers sell candles. Paraffin wax was first time used in 1854. These days also candles are made of paraffin wax.

Previously candles made by Burmah Oil Co. Ltd and Indo Burma Petroleum Industries were imported and in India candles were made out of stearin.

PLANT ECONOMICS OF NON-DRIP CANDLE MAKING

Rated Plant Capacity = 500.00 Kg/Day

LAND & BUILDING (Land Area 200 Sq.mt.) = Rs.1,65,000.00

PLANT & MACHINERY

1. Melting pot of aluminium
2. Moulds
3. Miscellaneous items i.e. Weighing scale, tools, buckets etc.

FIXED CAPITAL

1. LAND & BUILDING	Rs.	1,65,000.00
2. PLANT & MACHINERY	Rs.	70,000.00
3. OTHER FIXED ASSETS	Rs.	20,000.00
TOTAL	Rs.	2,55,000.00

RAW MATERIALS

1. Paraffin wax
2. Stearic Acid
3. Perfumes like sandalwood camphor
4. Wicks
5. Magnesium sulfate
6. Dextrin
7. Packaging (Paper Packets) materials

TOTAL WORKING CAPITAL/MONTH

1. RAW MATERIAL	Rs.	4,38,125.00
2. SALARY & WAGES	Rs.	13,920.00
3. UTILITIES & OVERHEADS	Rs.	23,300.00
TOTAL	Rs.	4,75,345.00

TOTAL CAPITAL INVESTMENT

TOTAL FIXED CAPITAL	Rs.	2,55,000.00
TOTAL WORKING CAPITAL FOR 2 MONTHS	Rs.	9,50,690.00
TOTAL	Rs.	12,05,690.00

TURN OVER/ANNUM

By selling of 1,50,000 kg. Candles	Rs.	75,00,000.00

PROFIT SALES RATIO = PROFIT / SALES X 100 = 21.58 %

RATE OF RETURN = OPERATING PROFIT / T.C.I X 100 = 134.21 %

BREAK EVEN POINT (B.E.P) = 18.05 %

30

CANDLE COATING

Coating on candles is being practised in the modern times so as to impart a glossy elegant and attractive look to the candle.

Coating of candles anehance customer's appeal which eventually given a phillip to this industry with novel innovative appearance.

This precisely account for increasing demand of coloured coated candles.

The candle making has been practised and despite the introduction of mass production methods, candles can still be made by well-established methods which require only simple equipment. Much of this equipment can be made by rural craftmen.

A candle is simply a solid cylinder of tallow, wax or other solid fat, containing a wick to give off light when burning. When the wick is lit, the flame radiates sufficient heat to melt a small pool of wax at the top of the candle. The liquid wax is then drawn up the wick by capailary action into the flame where it is vapourised and burnt. The size of the flame is important and should be related to the diameter of the candle.

If the wick used is too thick, it will cause, a large flame which generates so much heat that it prevents the formation of the bowl of molten fuel by melting the outer edge. On the other hand, if a wick which is too small is used,the small flame cannot generate enough heat to form a proper reservoir of molten fuel, as the heat radiated will not reach the edge of the candle until it is so far down that it will go out through lack of oxygen. The wick size, therefore, must be related to the diameter of the candle (as well as to the type of fuel). Although a rough guide to wick size is given later on in this profile, the only was is to provide a good candle is by trial and error.

The main purpose of the wax is to provide the fuel for the flame so the burning characteristics of the wax are extremely important. A good candle wax should produce a candle which burns steadily, lasts for a long time, produces very little, smoke and gives a good quality light. In addition, candle wax has other functions. It must be rigid enough to support the wick in a vertical position; it must be suitable for processing by one of the various candle making techniques; and it must look attractive.

Uses & Applications

Coated candles of different sizes, colour and designs can be manufactured for higher sales. Candles play great importance and are used mainly on festivals like Deepawali and Christmas. Candles in huge amount are sold mainly in festivals for illumination purposes. People use candles of different design and shapes as decoration pieces.

These are also widely used in villages where people face shortage of electricity and are also used in cities for lighting during electricity shortage or break down period. Artistic candles find use in big hotels, restaurants, clubs, churches and Kothies & Bunglows inspite of their high cost. These candles are of a good quality and finish and give very good flame. This type of candles does not bend also at the time of burning and therefore preferred.

It is more beneficial to make artistic candles than making ordinary candles for greater market in big cities but for smaller cities and villages, ordinary and improved quality of candles are of great use even and to an ordinary man as well as rich persons.

MANUFACTURING PROCESS

Candle Coating:-

Formulation:-

		Parts/wt.	*% age*
Stearic Acid	–	25	22.72
Paraffin wax	–	75	68.16
Sudan Colour	–	0.05	0.04
Staybelite Ester (Modifier for paraffin wax)	–	10	9.08
		110.05	100%

Process

Dissolve 0.05 parts of sudan colour in a melt of 25 parts stearic acid and add a melt of 75 parts paraffin wax in a tank with heating arrangement & stirrer also adds stabelite ester (Hydrogenated rosin ester) in the mix where extreme fasteners of light; sublimation and aging is required 2 parts of fast candle colour is used instead of 0.05 parts sudan colour.

* Modifier for paraffin waxes; The inclusion of staybelite ester in paraffin waxer increase their gloss transparancy and adhesion to various substrate.

** Stabelite Ester (Hydrogenated Rosin ester).

PLANT ECONOMICS OF COATING OF DIFFERENT SIZE & SHAPE

Rated Plant Capacity = 2500.00 Nos./Day

LAND & BUILDING (Land Area 300 sq.mtrs.) = Rs. 6,50,000.00

PLANT & MACHINERY

1. Mild Steel Dipping tank with stirrer & motor
2. Coating solution preparation tank with stirrer & heating arrangement
3. Raw material storage tanks
4. Pipe & Pipes fittings
5. Miscellaneous Equipments viz. motor heating equipments
6. Kettle for melting paraffin wax & stearic acid with heating arrangement

FIXED CAPITAL

1. LAND & BUILDING	Rs.	6,50,000.00
2. PLANT & MACHINERY	Rs.	90,000.00
3. OTHER FIXED ASSETS	Rs.	45,000.00
TOTAL	Rs.	7,85,000.00

RAW MATERIALS

1. Candle of different size & shape
2. Stearic Acid
3. Paraffin wax
4. Sudan Colours
5. Staybelite Ester (Hydrogenated-Rosin Ester)
6. Misc. Packaging materials (L.S.) etc

TOTAL WORKING CAPITAL/MONTH

1. RAW MATERIAL	Rs.	1,33,169.68
2. SALARY & WAGES	Rs.	49,125.00
3. UTILITIES & OVERHEADS	Rs.	38,200.00
TOTAL	Rs.	2,20,494.68

TOTAL CAPITAL INVESTMENT

TOTAL FIXED CAPITAL	Rs.	7,85,000.00
TOTAL WORKING CAPITAL FOR 3 MONTHS	Rs.	6,61,484.04
TOTAL	Rs.	14,46,484.04

TURN OVER/ANNUM

Receipt By sale of coated candles of different size shape & colours 750000 Nos.	Rs.	33,75,000.00

PROFIT SALES RATIO = PROFIT / SALES X 100 = 14.10 %

RATE OF RETURN = OPERATING PROFIT / T.C.I X 100 = 32.91 %

BREAK EVEN POINT (B.E.P) = 58.55 %

31

Suppliers of Machinery

Adarsh Engineers
15/25/1, Mangolpurkalan sec-2
Rohini, Near Jain Sweets,
Delhi-110085
9717814180, 8860524800
adarshengineeringwork@gmail.com

PRO-MLIN
Adress: Surcinska 179Dj,
New Belgrade, Belgrade,
Serbia (44.799877, 20.343291)
Phone: +38111/22-61-585
E-mail: promlin.rs@gmail.com
Nikola Petrašinovic : +381653000086

AUM ENTERPRISE
Factory : C/o. Aum Glass Compound,
8/B Gondal Road National Highway,
Behind Bimal Tyre, Kotharia,
RAJKOT.
Gujarat. INDIA
Cell : 0091 9824075654
Email : cmdetroja@gmail.com
Web : www.oilmachinery.com

RGK Group
Head Office :
Plot No. G - 1205, GIDC Lodhika,
Metoda, Rajkot, Gujarat,
India - 360035.
Phone: +91-2827-287414 / 101 / 102
Fax: +91-2827-287413
Web: http://www.rgkgroup.co.in/
Chairman
Mr. Ramnik Kotecha
Email ID : rgkotecha@gmail.com
Mobile : +91-9825075506

MEGHA GROUP OF COMPANIES
Mr. Gaurav Agarwal
10th Mile, Mawsmai,
District - Ri-Bhoi,
Khanapara, Meghalaya, India
Mobile: +91-9085165161
+91-9864091229
08042756255
meghaho108@gmail.com
http://www.meghagroup.co.in

Laxmi Narayan Pannalal
Mr. Ajay Kumar Rungta
Station Road, Navgachiya, Bhagalpur,
Bhagalpur - 853204, Bihar, India
Mobile: +91-9934880685

Aum Enterprise
Chetan Bhai Detroja(Proprietor)
5, Vishva Nagar,
Opposite Nil Madhav,
Near Patel Boarding Mavdi Plot,
Kothariya, Rajkot - 360004, Gujarat, India
Mobile: +91-9824075654

Shri Balaji Enterprises
Nitin Sharma(Owner)
No. 120, Gaushala,
Nadi Road, Laddhawala,
Muzaffarnagar - 251002, Uttar Pradesh, India
Mobile: +91-9997115416,
91-9997125226

Gayathri Match Industries
P. N. Senthil Kumar(Proprietor)
S. F. No. 28/1, Pattanam Pudur,
Pattanam, Coimbatore - 641016,
Tamil Nadu, India
Mobile: +91-9943027204
+91-9585527203
Phone: +91-422-2272047
+91-422-2270770

Jamal Engg. Works
Satish Kumar Saini(Manager)
No. 245/20, Kailash Colony,
Near ITI Gate, Sonipat - 131001,
Haryana, India
Mobile: +91-9896350438
+91-9992312355

Royal Paper Industries
SK Singh(Proprietor)
D-9, Ground Floor,
Manohar Park, Ashok Park,
Main Metro Station,
Delhi - 110026, India
Mobile: +91-9599905124
+91-9810601187
Phone: +91-11-28311013
91-11-28311014

Sonni Traders
Priya (Supervisor)
Shop No. 220, Shivaji Market,
Tagore Garden Extension,
Delhi - 110027, India
Mobile: +91-9718987876
+91-8860899309
Phone: +91-11-25103814

Super Tech Machinery Industries
Ranjeet Singh(Proprietor)
401, 4th Floor, Building Name Big Jobs
Netaji Subhash Place,
Pitampura, New
Delhi - 110034, Delhi, India
Mobile: +91-8860220098
+91-8860652826

B. K. Solution Pvt. Ltd.
Adarsh Vihar, New Bangali Tola, Opposite Of Chanakya Law College, Mithapur Bus Stand,
Patna-800001, Bihar, India
Biru Kumar (CEO)
Mobile: 08079467121

Gurap Industries
Sagar Gurap(Proprietor)
Shop No. 15, Navjeevan Tower,
OT Section, Opp. Jaslok School,
Below Union Bank ATM,
Camp No. 3 Uhasnagar West

District -Thane,
Ulhasnagar, Mumbai - 421003,
Maharashtra, India
Mobile: +91-9220550601
+91-8149550601
Phone: +91-251-6482266

R. K. Steel Engineering Works
Ram Niwas Sharma(Owner)
C - 79, Sainik Nagar,
Nawada Metro Station,
Uttam Nagar, Najafgarh Road,
Delhi - 110059, India
Mobile: +91-9810738060
+91-9717841299

Jogi Engineering Industries
Ajit Singh Dhaliwal (Proprietor)
No. 12/2, Ashwath Katte Road,
Kasturiba Nagar Near Old Tollgate,
Mysore Road, Bengaluru - 560026,
Karnataka, India
Mobile: +91-9341969693
Phone: +91-80-26744728
+91-80-26751822
Fax: +91-80-26741791

S.K. Industries
Naved Ahmad (Proprietor)
102, Garden City,
Opp. HDFC Bank,
Pawan Vihar Colony Gate
Near Akash Tower,
Almadina Hospital,
Bisalpur Chouraha,
University Road, Bareilly - 243005,
Uttar Pradesh, India
Mobile: +91-8755011715
+91-9319933241

Guniya Enterprises
WP, Wazirpur, New Delhi- 110052,
Mobile: +91-971-661-6630
guniyaenterprises@gmail.com

MOULDS/DIES FOR CANDLES

Shri Vaishno Enterprises
Sheoraj Singh Solanki(Director)
A 213, Shanti Gopal Chamber,
Shop No. 114,
Gali No. 1 Shakarpur,
Near Laxmi Nagar Metro Station,
New Delhi - 110092, Delhi, India
Mobile: +91-9899057451
+91-9711584258
Phone: +91-11-49076497

Jogi Engineering Industries
Ajit Singh Dhaliwal(Proprietor)
No. 12/2, Ashwath Katte Road,
Kasturiba Nagar Near Old Tollgate,
Mysore Road, Bengaluru - 560026,
Karnataka, India
Mobile: +91-9341969693
Phone: +91-80-26744728
+91-80-26751822
Fax: +91-80-26741791

CS Tools & Alloys
Janisirani S(Proprietor)
Plot No. 4, Senthil Nagar,
Mudichur Road Tambaram,
Chennai - 600063,
Tamil Nadu, India
Mobile: +91-9962156251
+91-9840676269

Devi Dayal & Company
Kapil Malik(Proprietor)
No. 18, Lal Kuan, Delhi - 110006,
India
Mobile: +91-9810044205
+91-9910044205
Phone: +91-11-23955271
+91-11-23945271
Fax: +91-11-23943690

Wasa Engineering Works
Azeem UR Rehman(Proprietor)
79/113 C, Bansmandi,
Police Chowki Road,
Kanpur - 208001,
Uttar Pradesh, India
Mobile: 8048555855

Varsha Candle Exporters
Ramesh (Manager)
Balaji Nagar, Ghatkesar,
Hyderabad - 501301,
Telangana, India
Mobile: +91-9848255385

Momentum Elastomers
Pragnesh Brahmbhatt (Proprietor)
Shade No. 97,
Kamal Industrial Estate,
Opposite Samit Hotel Bombay Conductor Road,
GIDC, Vatva,
Ahmedabad - 382445,
Gujarat, India
Mobile: +91-9374606470
+91-9825880842

Lakshmi Metal Industries
Deepak Sahni(CEO)
No. 27, Old Geeta Colony,
Near Punjab Sind Bank, Delhi - 110031, India
Mobile: 08079456199

32

Suppliers of Raw Materials

WAX

Dhruvika Chemicas Trading Private Limited
G P Singh(Sales & Marketing)
304, Swasti House,
70, Kazi Sayed Street Masjid,
Mumbai - 400003,
Maharashtra, India
Mobile: +91-8879943604
+91-8291895808
Phone: +91-22-40126821
+91-22-23454435
Fax: +91-22-27801853

Triveni Chemicals
K. K. Singh(Managing Director)
No. 135, Pancharatna Char Rasta
G. I. D. C., Vapi - 396195,
Gujarat, India
Mobile: +91-9227070667
Phone: +91-260-6618618
+91-260-6618624

Excel International
Sachin Bhuta(CEO)
B-610, Ghanshyam Enclave,
Link Road Near Lalji Pada Police Station,
Kandivali West, Mumbai - 400067,
Maharashtra, India
Mobile: +91-9322242840
+91-9769094794
Phone: +91-22-28675353
Fax: +91-22-28675353

Kaushik Agencies
Srinivasa Rao (Owner)
D. No. 2-42, Sector 6,
MVP Colony,
Visakhapatnam - 530027,
Andhra Pradesh, India
Mobile: +91-8008099567
+91-9248799567

First Rate Paper Solution
Ram Mahawar(Proprietor)
Shop No. 848, Daliganj,
Lucknow - 226001,
Uttar Pradesh, India
Mobile:+91-8090465680

Indian Wax Industries
Manager (Manager)
14-16 Narainrao Kohli Marg, 3
Mahavir Darshan,
Mumbai - 400003,
Maharashtra, India
Mobile: +91-9820025455
Phone: +91-22-23424870
+91-22-23422673

Sundry Enterprise
Teresa Francis (Proprietor)
E 42 Shankar Baug Society,
Nr Yogeshwar Park,
Tarsali Road, Vadodara - 390009,
Gujarat, India
Mobile: +91-9558729737

CANDLE WICKS/THREADS

Chetwani Brothers
Rakesh Chetwani (CEO)
D-57-A, 5th Road, Sardar Sahakari
Udyog Nagar Ajwa Road,
Vadodara - 390019, Gujarat, India
Mobile: +91-9824536638
Phone: +91-265-2561945

Abhishek Enterprises
Abhishek Bansal (Proprietor)
A 112, DSIIDC, Industrial Area,
Narela, Bawana Industrial Area,
Delhi - 110040, India
Mobile: +91-9999993971

Suryakiran Candle
Mohammad Rafiq(Proprietor)
House No. 1128/J/590,
Nandanvan Road,Hasan Bagh,
Nagpur - 440002,
Maharashtra, India
Mobile: +91-9371404842
+91-9284922633

Srethiya & Company
Thenmozhi Anandan(Proprietor)
Near Stedford Hospital,
Ambattur, Chennai - 600053,
Tamil Nadu, India
Mobile: +91-9841088442
+91-9841041689
Phone: +91-44-26582085

Sri Balaji Agencies
K. Balaji (Proprietor)
No. 133-A, Chitraikkara Street,
Madurai - 625001,
Tamil Nadu, India
Mobile: +91-9843052613
+91-9894151245
Phone: +91-452-2321760

Agnaye Exports Pvt. Ltd.
Kaushik Patel(Director)
Plot No. 4/5, Sector 2A,
Near Swami Temple Gandhi Nagar,
Ahmedabad - 382424,
Gujarat, India
Mobile: 8048013567

Lakshmi Candles
C Harish Kumar(Ceo)
No. 143/A, Avalahalli,
BSK 3rd Stage,
Bengaluru - 560085,
Karnataka, India
Mobile: 08048105744

Paramount Thread Works
Hitesh Shah (Proprietor)
No. 11/B, Purnima Building,
3rd Floor M. G. Road,
Mulund West,
Mumbai - 400080,
Maharashtra, India
Mobile: 08048008529

Threads Technology (India)
Mahesh M. Bapat (Director)
Mrs. Madura M Bapat
Unit No. 406,
Retiwala Industrial Estate,
Premises Co-Operative Society Limited,
Chinchpokli Cross
Lane No. 2, Byculla,
Mumbai - 400027,
Maharashtra, India
Mobile: 08079463958

Simco Thread Mills
Manager (Manager)
New No.20, Old No.17,
New Manickam St, Kosapet,
Purasaiwakkam,
Chennai-600007, Tamil Nadu, India
Mobile: +91-9843147380

Samarth Enterprises
Dattare Bhange
KBM Compound, Shop No. L 13-1,
Opposite Ashok Nagar
C. T. S. No. 23,
Marol Military Road, Andheri East,
Mumbai - 400059,
Maharashtra, India
Mobile: +91-9820768025

ALL FOLLOWING PROJECT REPORTS ARE READILY AVAILABLE

LEATHER & LEATHER PRODUCTS

- Handmade Leather
- Leather Auxillaries & Chemicals
- Leather Dyes
- Leather Washers
- Leather Board From Leather Waste
- Leather For Upholstry(Sofa)
- Leather Finishing Lacquer (Nitrocellulose Lacquer For Leather)
- Leather Garments
- Leather Goods
- Leather Shoes
- Leather Shoe & Chappal
- Leather Suitcases, Briefcases & Travelling Bags
- Leather Goods And Garments
- Leather Garments, Shoe & Chappal
- Leather Pigment Used For Colouring Of Leather
- Leather Tanning
- Leather Tanning & Garments (Eou)
- Sheep Skin Pickling Plant
- Shoe Upper
- Sport Shoes (Plastic)

MISCELLANEOUS PRODUCTS

- Agarbatti (Insence Stick)
- Abrasive Paper
- Agarbatti (Mosquito Repellent)
- Agarbati Bamboo Stick
- Agarbatti Synthetic Perfumery Compound
- Air Freshner(Odonil Type)
- Air Taxi
- Amusement Park
- Anodic Aluminium Label
- Aquaculture Prawn Farming (100% Eou)
- Aqua Culture Shrimp Farming (100% Eou)
- Artificial Flowers
- Artificial Jewellery
- Asbestos Yarn
- Ash Trays For Maruti Vehicle
- Air Bubble Packaging
- Asphaltic Roofing Sheet (Metal Components)
- Automatic Book Binding
- Alkyd Resin
- Apple Juice Concentrate
- Ball Point Pen Fefills (Jotter Type)
- Bank Branch Building
- Banquet Hall
- Bio-Coal Briquettes From Agriculturalcellulose Waste
- Boot Cream/Polish
- Buffing & Polishing Compound
- Brass Badges By Etching
- Briquetted Fuel From Agro Waste
- Briquetting Of Lignite Coal
- Buffalo Horn Tip, Hoof
- Banquet Hall
- Button
- Calcined Petroleum (C.P) Coke
- Canvas Shoes
- Canvas Shoes, Jungle Boots
- Carbon Brush, Brush Holder & Slip Ring
- Cement Sheets With Coir Fibre & Other Segments
- Ceramic Tiles (Glazed) By Double Firing/Heating
- Children Recreation Centre
- Coal Briquettes
- Cold Storage & Ice
- Cold Storage For Fruits And Vegetables
- Compressor (Hermetic) For Air Conditioner
- Costume Jewellery/Imitation Jewellery
- Decorative Laminated Sheet (Sunmica)
- Dental Colleges
- Diamond Cutting & Exports
- Drinking Straw From Propylene
- Engineering College
- Engineering College, Management Institute, Cbse School, Hostel (Boys And Girls), Medical College With Hospital And Research Institute
- Electropolishing On Gold Jewellery (Gold Ornaments)
- Entertainment Club
- Fashion Technology Institute
- Fast Food Parlour
- Fast Food (Instant Food & Fast Food Parlour)
- Fire Extinguishers (Soda Acid Type)
- Fish Net
- Floriculture (Cut Flower Rose) With Green House
- Floor Covering Sheet
- Film Studio (Video)
- Flush Door, Chip Board, Wood Wool & Other Insulating Boards
- Gas Detectors Of L.P.G
- Gems Manufacturing
- Glass Bottle By Scrap
- Glass Jars Manufacturing Plant For Packaging Of 50, 100, 150, 200 Grams Coffee Packaging
- Goat & Sheep Farming
- Gold Electroplating
- Gold Jewellery (E.O.U)
- Gold Plated Silver Jewellery & Cutlery
- Granite Slab And Tiles
- Granite Mining
- Green House
- Hard Chromium Plating
- Health Club And Beauty Parlour Cum Hair
- Saloon With Sona Bath
- Health Club Cum Beauty Parlour Training Institute
- Horn Tip,Hoove Button
- Hospital

EIRI

is fully capable to prepare any Project Report of your Choice

- Hospital (100 Beds)
- Hospital (200 Beds)
- Ice Making Plant
- Imitation And Costume
- Jewellery (Necklace, Earrings Ear Top Etc.)
- Initmate Scent Chemicals From All Types Of Flavour
- Investment Casting
- Jute, Coir, Glass Rope/ Sutli
- Jute Twine
- Jute Bags From Yarn Without Spinning Process
- L.P.G Bottling Plant
- L.P.G Regulator (Domestic Purpose)
- Laminated Particle Board & Hard Board
- Laminated Safety & Toughened Glass
- Leasing & Hire Purchase
- Lichen (Charila)
- Manila Ropes
- Medical College
- Medical University
- Metal Pretreatment Chemicals Powder, Coating Chemicals
- Match Unit From Waxed Paper
- Medium Density Fibre Board
- Melamine Crockery
- Mineral Water
- Mini Cement Plant
- Mirror Silver, Golden, Pink, Black & Smokes
- Modern Advt. Agency With Dtp & Film Studio
- Motel/Small Hotel
- Multi Colour Printing
- Multi Purpose Cold Storage And Dehydration And Canning Of Fruits And Vegetables
- Multi Storey Commercial Complex Alongwith Residential And Delux Flats For Foreign Tourists & Revolving Restaurent At The Top
- Multiple Lamination Industry
- Mushroom Growing And Processing (By Deep Freezing Method)
- News Paper Printing
- Nickel Lined Industrial Screen
- Non Coking Coal To Coking Coal
- Nursing Home
- Offset Colour Printing Press (Six Colour)

Market Survey Cum Detailed Techno Economic Feasibility Report on all Projects are available Contact.
"ENGINEERS INDIA RESEARCH INSTITUTE". 4449, Nai Sarak (D), Main Road, Delhi-110006 (India)
Ph. : 09811437895, 91-11-23918117, 23916431, 45120361, 64727385 Fax : 91-11-23916431
E-mail : eiriprojects@gmail.com, eiribooks@yahoo.com • website: www.eiri.in, www.eiriindia.org

ALL FOLLOWING PROJECT REPORTS ARE READILY AVAILABLE

PAINT, ENAMEL, SOLVENTS, THINNERS, INKS & VARNISH

PAINT, ENAMEL, SOLVENTS, THINNERS, INKS & VARNISH

- Acrylic Emulsion Paints
- Acrylic Cement Paint (Dry Powder)
- Aluminium Paint
- Automobile Paints
- Ball Point Pen Refill Ink
- Bituminious Road Emulsion
- Bitumen
- Bituminious Felts For Water & Damp Proofing
- Bituminious Road Emulsion Rapid Medium & Slow Setting
- Buffing & Polishing
- Cement Paint For White & Grey Cement
- Dispersant
- Dry Distemper
- Dry Distemper & Cement Paint
- Duplicating Ink Black For Gestner Duplicator
- Emulsion Paints (Water Based)
- Hammertone Paint
- Insulating Varnish & Wire Enamel
- Iron Oxide Pigments
- Insulating Varnish (Poly Vinyl Butyral Based, Ffc Grade)
- Lime Colour (Cement Colour)
- Synthetic Red Oxide For Floorings
- Solvent & Thinners
- Marking Inks (Water Proof)
- Metal Naphthanate (As Drier For Paints)
- N.C.Putty
- Offset Printing Ink
- Oil Bound Distemper Paint
- Paint Brushes
- Paint Manufacture For Rolling Coating Of Aluminium And Steel Coil
- Paint Removers
- Paint Industry
- Paint & Varnish
- Picture Varnish
- Powder Coating Paint
- Printing Inks (Offset,Flexo & Roto Gravure)
- Primer Paint & Enamel Paint
- Putty & Water Proofing Paint
- Printing Inks (Flexo-Graphic Ink)
- Putty (Metal Casement)
- Red Oxide Primer (Anti Corrosive)
- Refrectory Paint (Graphite Based)
- Screen Printing Inks
- Silk Screen Printing Ink Formulation For Plastic, Paper, Cloth
- Stamp & Pad Ink
- Stoving Paint
- Spirit Soluble Maleic Resin
- Texture Paint
- Thinners And Its Allied Products
- Toner Ink
- Varnish Thinner (Solvent)
- Vacuum Metallizing Lacquers
- Wood Primer

PHARMACEUTICAL, DRUGS, AYURVEDIC/HERBAL COSMETICS & MEDICINES, HOMOEOPATHIC MEDICINES, HOMOEOPATHIC MEDICINES, DISPOSABLE SYRINGE, DENTAL COLLEGE & FINE CHEMICALS ETC.

MEDICINES, HOMOEOPATHIC MEDICINES, DISPOSABLE SYRINGE, DENTAL COLLEGE & FINE CHEMICALS ETC.

- Aromatic Pills
- Alumina From Bauxite
- Aspirin
- Ayurvedic Pain Balm Ointments
- Ayurvedic Churan And Tablets
- Ayurvedic Tablets (Hajmola Type)
- Ayurvedic/Herbalpharmacy
- Ayurvedic Sherbats
- Ayurvedic Products
- Bulk Drugs (E.O.U)
- Blood Bags
- Calcium Gluconate
- Capsule, Tablet & Injection With Modern Instruments
- Cashew Feni
- Chloroquinone Phosphate (Bulk Drugs)
- Clinical Thermometer
- Dental Clinic
- Dental College
- Dental Grade Eugenol
- Dextrose Monohydrate, Liquid Glucose
- Dehydrated Onion & Onion Powder
- Dextrose Powder (Anhydrous From Starch)
- Dextrose Saline Solution
- Distillery (I.M.F.L)
- Disposable Needles For Syringes
- Disprin
- Distilled Water
- Empty Hard Gelatine Capsules
- Fairness Cream
- Filling & Packing Of Capsules
- Glucose - D - Powder
- Glycerine
- Hair Colour Mate (Formulations And Process Only)
- Herbal Cosmetics
- Herbal Shampoo
- Herbal Shampoo And Cream
- Herbal Hair Oils (Ayurvedic)
- Homoe & Bio-Medicines With Mother Tincture
- Homoepathic Medicines
- Hypodermic Needles
- I.V. Fluids
- Ibuprofen
- Infusion & Transfusion Sets (I.V. Set)
- Injectable For Pharmaceuticals
- Injection Ampoules Packaging Box
- Integerated Surgical Cotton
- Ice Making Plant
- Ice & Cold Storage
- Lactose & By Products Processing From Milk
- Lichen (Jatamansi Charila)
- Liquid Glucose And Its By-Products
- L-Lysine Monohydro Chloride
- Liquid Glucose From Potatoes
- Medical College
- Methanol (Hpcl Grade)
- Nicotine From Tobacco Waste
- Ointment-Ayurvedic (Yellow & White)
- Pharmaceutical And Food Grade Gelatine
- Pharmaceutical Industry (Tablets, Capsules, Liquid, Gel, Ointment Powder Injectable)
- Pharmaceutical Unit (Eou) With Formulations, Injectables, Etc.
- Pyridine & Derivatives
- Salt (Iodized Salt)
- Saline & Injection Water
- Saline Water & Dextrose Solution (I.V.Fluid In Plastic Bottles)
- Sorbitol
- Starch (Maize)
- Surgical Adhesive Plaster
- Surgical Bandages
- Surgical Gloves
- Surgical Cotton
- Surgical Cotton And Bandage
- Synthetic Camphor Powder
- Tablets & Capsules
- Tissue Culture
- Tincture From Rectified Spirit
- Trimethopime
- Veterinary College With Hospital
- Veterenary Medicines (Only Formulations)
- Vitamin 'C', Sorbitol' Anhydrous Dextrose, Starch

Market Survey Cum Detailed Techno Economic Feasibility Report on all Projects are available Contact.
"ENGINEERS INDIA RESEARCH INSTITUTE". 4449, Nai Sarak (D), Main Road, Delhi-110006 (India)
Ph. : 09811437895, 91-11-23918117, 23916431, 45120361, 64727385 Fax : 91-11-23916431
E-mail : eiriprojects@gmail.com, eiribooks@yahoo.com • website: www.eiri.in, www.eiriindia.org